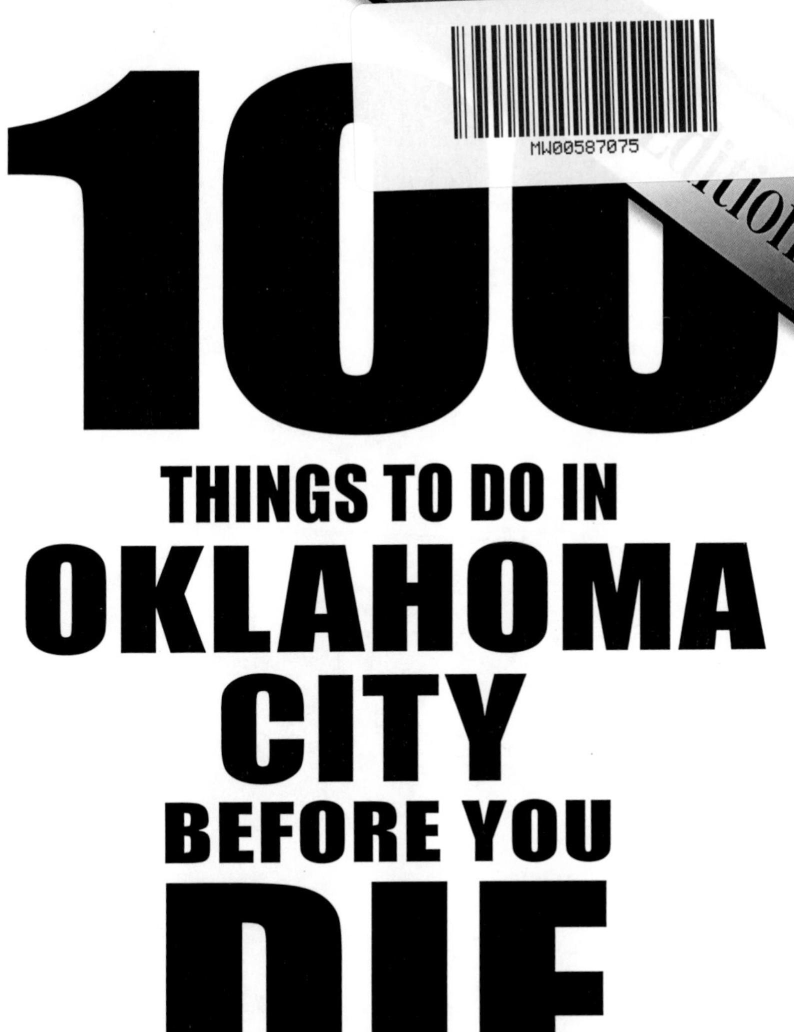

100 THINGS TO DO IN OKLAHOMA CITY BEFORE YOU DIE

17
18
19

100 THINGS TO DO IN OKLAHOMA CITY BEFORE YOU DIE

2nd Edition

LAUREN ROTH

Reedy Press
PO Box 5131
St. Louis, MO 63139, USA
www.reedypress.com

Library of Congress Control Number: 2018936116

ISBN: 9781681061450

Cover Image: Courtesy of RIVERSPORT Rapids
Author Headshot: James Adams

Design by Jill Halpin

Printed in the United States of America
22 23 5 4 3 2

Please note that websites, phone numbers, addresses, and company names are subject to change or cancellation. We did our best to relay the most accurate information available, but due to circumstances beyond our control, please do not hold us liable for misinformation. When exploring new destinations, please do your homework before you go.

DEDICATION

To Elizabeth.

Photo courtesy of OKC Zoo

CONTENTS

Music and Entertainment

Sports and Recreation

Culture and History

PREFACE

Welcome to the Big Friendly!

Maybe it's the ease in which one can move from one end of the city to the other, the abundance of sunny days, an affordable quality of life, or just something in its collective DNA—everything about Oklahoma City is friendly, welcoming, and above all, glad you're here.

Despite having grown up here and seeing its remarkable evolution, I still discover something new (or old) every week, from new restaurants and music venues to exciting urban repurposing of formerly neglected or abandoned structures. This is a city that doesn't hesitate to reinvent itself.

Narrowing down the thousands of things anyone would enjoy doing in Oklahoma City to the 100 things contained in this book isn't as easy as it sounds. Just when you think you've got your list, something new comes along to deserve a spot among the 100.

Where does one even start? With food, of course. This guide will introduce you to many legendary eateries that have deliciously stood the test of time, as well as several new (and equally noteworthy) stops along your culinary journey through the city. If your idea of a taste adventure involves local beer, this book will point you the right way to explore one of the city's booming industries: craft brewing.

This guide will also ensure that you find plenty of entertainment, music, and recreational activities to make the most of your visit. Music is essential to an Oklahoman existence; new music venues abound, but you'll find countless holes-in-the-wall where you can hear incredibly accomplished musicians perform live.

Oklahoma City also enjoys four distinct seasons, and most days lend themselves to outdoor experiences the whole family can enjoy. In addition to some itineraries by season, we've included several "insider" tips to make your visit even better.

Keep this guide with you as a starting point for some retail therapy, too! Oklahoma City is home to hundreds of unique, locally-owned shops and boutiques that will not disappoint even the most seasoned shopper. As you'll read in the Shopping section, many local retailers also support community-focused nonprofits by donating a portion of sales, which means your purchases help others in need.

Think of the 100 things listed in this guide as the tip of a much, much bigger iceberg as you're planning your time in Oklahoma City. It truly is impossible to condense all the city has to offer within the pages of this book, so if you discover something you think should make the next 100 Things list, please let me know!

Photo courtesy of American Banjo Museum

ACKNOWLEDGMENTS

You've probably heard the term "football widows," wives whose husbands disappear every year for months at a time during football season. For every writer, I think there must be dozens of "writer widows/widowers," too—the people who support you in the background without complaining about being abandoned when publishing deadlines loom.

Topping that list are my kids, Reynolds, Templin, and Jennings, three of the loveliest humans on the planet, despite growing up around non-stop publishing deadlines. Thank you for not setting the house on fire.

Thank you to my husband and number one cheerleader, Eric, who provided home-cooked meals and encouragement during marathon writing days and who refused to go to bed if I was still writing.

Thank you to the fantastic team at Reedy Press for your skilled editing and project management.

Thank you to the Oklahoma City Convention and Visitors Bureau, the Greater Oklahoma City Chamber, and to the many retail and entertainment friends who so graciously provided several images for this book.

Above all, thank you to my mom and dad, the first people who told me, "You should write a book one day."

Cathy Cummings, owner, Vito's Ristorante
Photo courtesy of Eric Roth

FOOD AND DRINK

1

ENJOY A ROOFTOP SUNSET
AT PACKARD'S NEW AMERICAN KITCHEN

Longtime Oklahoma City restaurateurs Robert Ross and Rusty Loeffler began their successful hospitality careers in 1971 as co-founders of Oklahoma's iconic Interurban restaurants, and they've been together ever since. Only conjoined twins spend more time together, so when the opportunity came to revive the long-forgotten Packard dealership building in midtown's Automobile Alley, the duo accepted the challenge together and Packard's New American Kitchen was born, giving local flavor to classic American dishes.

One of the hallmarks of Packard's something-for-everyone menu is its locally sourced fare (honey, peaches, free-range chicken, local beers) that varies according to the season. From the beer-battered crab beignets to the blackened redfish, seasonal cocktails, and the Nutella cheesecake mousse, Packard's touches all the culinary bases for lunch, dinner, and a wildly popular weekend brunch (read: mimosas served in carafes) on Saturdays and Sundays. What could be better? If it's nice outside, take your dining experience to the next level on Packard's rooftop bar, where you'll enjoy a fantastic view of the downtown skyline. (Closed Mondays.)

201 NW 10th St., Oklahoma City
(405) 605-3771
packardsokc.com

2

CLASSIC DINING
AT JUNIOR'S SUPPER CLUB

Entering Junior's Supper Club is like walking into a time warp back to its 1970s origins as an elite, private dinner club and cocktail bar. Its original, speakeasy décor, low ceilings, and sunken piano bar serve as visual reminders of Oklahoma City's oil boom heyday. To change them now would incite an uproar among the legions of loyal patrons who insist, "If it ain't broke…"

If you ask a local where you can find a great steak, Junior's (open for lunch and dinner) will always come up among the top three of OKC's surf and turf restaurants. They consistently serve one of the best steak and lobster meals you'll find, but the fried chicken and white gravy will absolutely set you free. Both the Caesar salad, prepared tableside, and Junior's brandy ice, are signature concoctions that draw the faithful masses into its dark red lair, which is weirdly ensconced in the basement of Oil Center West in northwest Oklahoma City. Live music, a smoking lounge, and a longtime professional wait staff create an intimate atmosphere that is unrivaled in this city.

2601 NW Expressway, Oklahoma City
(405) 848-5597
juniorsokc.com

3

GET YOUR FANCY PANTS
TO THE MULE

If you've only got one day in OKC, make sure that day involves lunch at The Mule, where comfort food is king in a realm of local brews and seasonal cocktails, all served in a supremely local and laid-back, pub-like atmosphere in the heart of the Plaza District.

Think of every possible spin on the time-honored grilled cheese and just know you'd still come up short in comparison to The Mule's extensive lineup of gourmet sandwich fare. Locals love the Macaroni Pony, a concoction of jalapeño cornbread, chipotle BBQ pulled pork, three-cheese mac and cheese, and pickles. You won't go wrong with the Fancy Pants: roasted chicken, brie, Gruyère, caramelized onion, sliced pear, basil pesto, and a balsamic reduction, served on Vienna wheat bread. Vegetarian or vegan? Go for the Herbivore.

The Mule's drink menu, generously splashed with local brews and staff-created cocktails, is equally revered for its inventiveness.

On the weekend, you'll probably have to wait for a table and you'll be glad to. If it's nice, sit outside and watch the locals meander through the Plaza District's main artery, NW 16th Street.

1630 N Blackwelder Ave., Oklahoma City
(405) 601-1400
themuleokc.com

4

STAKE YOUR CLAIM
AT CATTLEMEN'S STEAKHOUSE

The iconic Cattlemen's Steakhouse (originally known as Cattlemen's Café) owes its renown to several distinguishing facts. It's been continuously operating as a landmark in historic Stockyards City since 1910, which makes it almost as old as statehood. It's been consistently voted one of the top steakhouses in the metro by locals. It once changed hands with a single roll in a game of dice.

Modest in both décor and price, Cattlemen's is the real deal. There's no need to put on airs when you're good at what you do; let's just say that an inferior steakhouse wouldn't last more than a lunch hour in the state's epicenter for beef. For more than a century, Cattlemen's has been a destination for its generous portions of corn-fed steak and lamb fries. It's not uncommon to see celebrities and everyday cowboys sitting side by side among the restaurant's loyal clientele.

Cattlemen's Steakhouse, 1309 S Agnew Ave.
(405) 236-0416
cattlemensrestaurant.com

GET IT WITH GRAVY
AT THE DRUM ROOM

The Drum Room describes itself as "Fine Fowl and Fixin's. Comfort food and kick ass bar for the soul." As a frequent, finger-licking consumer of all of the above, I'm inclined to agree.

Against a backdrop of drums décor (repurposed drums make fantastic pendant lights!) and a full bar with rotating features, The Drum Room zeros in on the things that matter most on a lunch or dinner menu (or in life, really), serving fresh-to-order fried chicken and waffles (or a biscuit, if you prefer), mashed potatoes and white country gravy, pimento cheeseburger, fried okra, and wings. You'll taste some heat in The Drum Room's chicken batter or in its famous pimento cheeseburger. Mitigate that heat with any one of The Drum Room's many craft and local beers, which, thanks to the bar's state-of-the-art refrigeration system, will be the coldest beer you'll find anywhere.

For a side dish of quirkiness that pays homage to the LP, you can bring your own vinyl albums to play while you enjoy dinner and drinks.

4309 N Western Ave., Oklahoma City
(405) 604-0990
drumroomokc.com

YOU'RE PART OF *LA FAMIGLIA* AT VITO'S RISTORANTE

Owner Cathy Cummings says that, for as long as she can remember, there's always been an Italian restaurant in the family. That translates to a lot of family recipes for exceptional Italian fare, which is what the charming Cathy has served to her Oklahoma City family since 2004 at Vito's.

Vito's is everything a family-owned-and-operated neighborhood Italian restaurant should be. When you arrive, Cathy will most likely be the one to call you by name and greet you with a hug, while simultaneously attending to the requests of thirty other patrons—typical of her warm, southern Italian heritage.

Many of the pasta dishes, including her heavenly lasagna, feature Cathy's own sugo, Italian red sauce, from her grandmother's recipe. All dishes on Vito's menu of Italian classics are prepared fresh, of course. Cathy's eggplant parmesan, chicken spedini, meatballs, and tiramisu are a great place to start.

Call ahead if you're going late in the week. Seating is limited.

7628 N. May Ave., Oklahoma City
(405) 848-4867
vitosokc.com

7

FRANCE MEETS OKC
AT LA BAGUETTE BISTRO

Equal parts bakery, boucherie, restaurant, and wine bar, La Baguette is the chic fusion of European and American cuisine made possible by Grenoble, France natives (and brothers) Michel and Alain Buthion.

Since 1988, the Brothers Buthion have been celebrated for their ability to bring an authentic taste of France, to OKC in the form of La Baguette's signature offerings—among them Croque Monsieur, crêpes, and quiche. Like all top-tier restaurants, La Baguette stands out for the quality that comes from hands-on owners who are passionate about what they do. The Buthions frequently make their way through the restaurant, chatting up regulars and first-timers alike.

If you manage to finish your lunch, dinner, or brunch without a visit to the bakery counter for freshly baked desserts or baguettes, check your pulse.

7408 N May Ave., Oklahoma City
(405) 840-3047
labaguettebistro.com

THE POPS ARE TOPS
AT POPS

Fill up both your tanks at this roadside must-see! Located a few minutes west of Oklahoma City along historic Route 66, Pops stands as an unmistakable salute to the gas stations of yesteryear, but with a modern twist—specifically its towering, sixty-six-foot- tall pop bottle (considered to be the world's tallest, but it's unclear whether there's a pop bottle height competition to begin with) made of color-changing LED rings.

Inside, Pops' décor consists of nearly seven hundred kinds of soda and bottled beverages across a floor-to-ceiling display of color and carbonation. In its well-stocked refrigerators, you'll find beverages you'd long forgotten, or that you never knew existed (Rowdy Roddy Piper Bubble Gum Soda, anyone?). Pops' Restaurant could stand on its own merit as a great stop for a burger, breakfast, hotdog, or milkshake. Whether you choose the Round Barn Burger (topped with fried egg, cheddar cheese, and smoked applewood bacon) or the Mother Road Omelet with biscuits and gravy, you'll never leave Pops on "E."

660 W Hwy. 66, Arcadia
(405) 928-7677
pops66.com

GET IT HOT
OFF THE PRESS

If the Plaza District's meteoric growth of excellent dining options had screeched to a halt two or three years ago, locals would still go to bed happy and satisfied, but they would have missed out on The Press, which opened its doors in the fall of 2017, taking its name from the building's previous incarnation as the Northside Press and replacing the telltale waft of ink with the come-hither whiff of comfort food.

Voted by readers as "Favorite New Restaurant" in *405 Magazine*'s "Best of the City" poll, The Press isn't just about candy apple bacon gravy (although no one would fault it if that were true) and house tots with cheese (heaven help us). Veggie burgers, quinoa oatmeal, beans and greens, and a lovely kale salad live in perfect harmony alongside the "official state dinner" (as adopted in 1988 by the Oklahoma State Legislature), consisting of BBQ pork, chicken-fried steak, fried okra, squash, corn, sausage gravy, strawberries, black-eyed peas, and pecan pie. The official state dinner is available every Tuesday after 4:00 p.m. I'd wear my elastic waistband, if I were you.

1610 N Gatewood Ave., Oklahoma City
(405) 208-7739
thepressokc.com

10

SCORE YOUR SWEET FIX
AT PIE JUNKIE

Local residents Darcy Schein and Leslie Coale-Mossman discovered their mutual love for cooking and baking during a play date with their kids. They soon began baking pies for local eateries, and just like their kids, their budding business grew nearly overnight. Now with a storefront in OKC's Plaza District, the dessert-loving duo bakes more than 20,000 pies every year. From what is arguably the metro's best key lime pie to their wildly popular strawberry rhubarb, Pie Junkie insists on fresh ingredients you can pronounce in each one of their made-from-scratch masterpieces.

There's always a slice waiting for you. If you need the whole pie (and we've all had those days), best to call ahead. Any way you slice it, you're bound to become a pie junkie, too, but you'll need to schedule your fix: Pie Junkie is closed Sundays and Mondays.

1711 NW 16th St., Oklahoma City
(405) 605-8767
piejunkie.com

THE BIRD IS THE WORD
AT EISCHEN'S BAR

For a quintessentially Oklahoman experience, it's well worth the thirty-minute drive from Oklahoma City to the state's oldest bar, Eischen's (est. 1896), in Okarche.

In a world of white table linens and culinary snobbery, Eischen's blithely celebrates exactly what it is: the hyper-rustic, deep-fried capital of chicken, okra, and everything else that's right in this world. Each week, nearly three thousand birds are fried to golden perfection, served whole, and modestly presented with a side of pickles and white bread.

Don't let the word "bar" discourage you from convening the entire family for a home-style lunch or dinner in the restaurant's lively, "silverware-is-for-sissies" atmosphere, featured on Food Network's *Diners, Drive-Ins and Dives*. Eischen's is usually crowded, but always family-friendly. If the experience doesn't remind you of Grandma's house on a Sunday afternoon, you probably need a new grandma.

109 N 2nd Street, Okarche
(405) 263-9939
eischensbar.com

12

HANG OUT WITH "THE CLIQUE"

AT FRIENDS BAR & GRILL

Just hear me out on this one—ordinarily, I wouldn't direct a reader into a bar for the sake of going to a bar. In this case, however, I'm making an exception.

There's nothing—and I mean nothing—fancy about Friends Bar & Grill. Adjust your expectations of ambience accordingly. It's a bar with most of the trappings: pool tables, shuffleboards, and TVs, but without much in the way of hard-to-find beverages. I can't even vouch for the grill. Still, this local bar, which adheres to a "smoke 'em if you've got 'em" policy (another deal-breaker in my book) attracts a full house that, admittedly, skews a bit older several nights a week because of one thing: a phenomenal house band called, appropriately, The Clique. Covering a gamut of musical styles and nailing Every. Last. One. of them, the band is worth a raise of your glass.

3705 W Memorial Rd., Ste. 604, Oklahoma City
(405) 751-4057
facebook.com/Friends-Bar-Grill-131371877016663

13

YOUR OKC RITE OF PASSAGE:
EDNA'S ORIGINAL LUNCHBOX

Hard to find, but impossible to forget, Edna's Club & Restaurant is the *grande dame* of iconic Oklahoma City dive bars, made famous by its late owner Edna Scott's original Lunchbox, a beer-based concoction of Coor's Light, amaretto, and orange juice, served in a frosted mug—not quite a Dreamsicle, but dreamy, nonetheless.

Since its accidental invention (by Edna) in the early 1990s, more than two million Lunchboxes have quenched the thirst of locals and out-of-towners alike, making it the undisputed favorite drink in dozens of "Best Of..." polls. And while the Lunchbox is an obvious "rite of passage" for first-timers to this tiny tavern with its dollar bill-covered walls, the same could be said for your entire Edna's experience, which comes with a great bar menu, an inviting back patio, a spirited neighborhood crowd, and a well-stocked jukebox that rocks until 2:00 am daily.

5137 N Classen Blvd., Oklahoma City
(405) 840-3339
ednasokc.com

GRAB A PINT
AT SEAN CUMMINGS' IRISH RESTAURANT

Owner and chef Sean Cummings' family has been rooted in the Emerald Isle for centuries, which lends even more authenticity to the convivial atmosphere of the neighborhood Sean Cummings' Irish Restaurant. Equally authentic are the family recipes that comprise its menu: shepherd's pie, bread pudding, bangers and mash, golden fried fish and chips, salad topped with steak and potatoes, and what Oklahoma City restaurant critic Steve Gill swears is the single best Reuben he's ever had, bar none.

But Irish restaurants and pubs cannot live on bread (pudding) alone; they need music. Sean Cummings keeps a full slate of singers and musicians whose nightly performances always include audience participation (even if that just means banging on the table during "Whiskey in the Jar"), ratcheting up the restaurant's friendly, public house vibe tenfold.

7628 N May Ave., Oklahoma City
(405) 841-7326
seancummings-ok.com

15

GO FROM FARM TO TABLE
AT WHISKEY CAKE KITCHEN AND BAR

Locally sourced farm ingredients are the mainstay of Whiskey Cake Kitchen and Bar's seasonally-influenced menu of classic American fare. In fact, the restaurant website boasts that everything from its main dishes to its handcrafted cocktails to its celebrated desserts is infused with available local ingredients. The overall vibe of Whiskey Cake is also decidedly local and rustic in a good way; servers, bartenders, and chefs are knowledgeable and passionate about the freshness of the ingredients in what they serve, so much so that they can tell you where today's basil came from, or where the tomatillos in the tomatillo salsa originated.

Whiskey Cake's bar is nicely stocked with hand-selected whiskeys purchased by the barrel in Kentucky every year. An equally abundant inventory of locally produced beers makes Whiskey Cake a go-to destination for after-work relaxation if the siren's song of the restaurant's namesake dessert, whiskey cake (a toffee forte, infused with bourbon anglaise, spiced pecans, and a side bowl of fresh whipped cream), doesn't draw you in first.

1845 Northwest Expy. (near Penn Square Mall), Oklahoma City
(405) 582-2253
whiskeycake.com

16

GET THE CAKE!

AT LEO'S BAR-B-Q

Asking a local about good barbecue can produce varied responses, depending on the age of the expert. Direct this inquiry to a native who looks like he/she hasn't missed many meals and you'll always be directed to Leo's Bar-B-Q, an Oklahoma City institution since 1974, long before it was featured on the Food Network's *Diners, Drive-Ins and Dives*. The pillars of this institution—Leo's ribs, brisket, bologna, and hot links--are sold in sandwiches, dinner portions, or by the pound (the way nature intended). Expect a fast-moving line during the busy lunch hour, when you might be seated with other diners to maximize the eating space.

As legendary as the late Leo himself is the restaurant's signature strawberry banana cake, a simple white sheet cake, lightly glazed with icing, and topped with strawberries and bananas. You'll smell intoxicatingly smoky when you leave Leo's, prompting locals to ask, "Did you get the cake?" You'll say yes, because you know your Leo's experience wouldn't be complete without it.

3631 N Kelley Ave., Oklahoma City
(405) 424-5367
facebook.com/LeosBarbecue

MEDITERRANEAN FLAVOR
AT BETHLEHEM MEDITERRANEAN GRILL

This is Alex Al-adass' third restaurant in the Oklahoma City metro. He first gained a cult following of Mediterranean food lovers with Camilya's in north OKC and Jerusalem Mediterranean Cuisine in neighboring Edmond. Al-adass has taken the show a few minutes farther up the road in Edmond with an expanded menu of made-to-order Mediterranean, Greek, and Middle Eastern offerings, which include several vegan, vegetarian, and gluten-free recipes.

Al-adass makes everything from scratch—nothing from cans. Everything is made in a traditional way, with no corners cut. The falafel is made fresh and never frozen. Bethlehem's hummus, made daily, is the smoothest and most flavorful around. (Be sure to ask for "Eric's Pretty Hummus," a secret menu item. No extra charge, just extra pretty.)

733 W Danforth Rd., Edmond
(405) 216-5124

COME HUNGRY
TO NIC'S GRILL

As long as carnivores love burgers, there will always be a line wrapped around this seventeen-seat burger joint, which is widely hailed as the home of Oklahoma City's best burger. Grilled to perfection, Nic's half-pounders are made to order: seared on both sides, slow-finished on a flat-top grill, and served in a traditional red burger basket with a scorching heap of fresh-cut curly fries. The restaurant's cameo on the Food Network's Diners, *Drive-Ins and Dives* may very well have increased its street cred with non-locals, but its legions of devotees will happily endure a longer wait time if that's what stands between them and their onion burger. Note: Nic's is cash only.

1201 N Pennsylvania Ave., Oklahoma City
(405) 524-0999

19

GET A SLICE OF HEAVEN
AT UPPER CRUST

During my many visits with family and friends to Upper Crust, no one in the party (child or adult) has ever been disappointed with their menu choice. Do start with the fried mozzarella, which is fresh and hand-breaded daily before it's delivered as molten, gooey nirvana with a heavenly marinara sauce. The Farmers' Market salad, heaped with Fuji apples, candied walnuts, gorgonzola, and arugula on Boston bibb lettuce, is as much a feast for the eyes as for the appetite. You will never go wrong with any pizza, but you can go slightly more right when crispy prosciutto is involved, namely, with the Numbers pizza, the number one choice of meat lovers. Equally decadent under the carnivore heading is the Knife and Fork Meatball Sub, the mere mention of which evokes an emotional response from my globe-trotting husband, who swears it's the best meatball on the planet. Upper Crust also boasts a constellation of adult beverage options that threaten to gild the culinary lily, but since you're already at the table, why not start with the Ultimate Bloody Mary?

Lucky for you, there are two metro locations:

5860 N Classen Blvd., Oklahoma City
(405) 842-7743

1205 NW 178th St., Edmond
(405) 285-8887

ucpizza.com

A CUT ABOVE:
BOULEVARD STEAKHOUSE

You're in Oklahoma: beef country. We will not let you down when it comes to steak. And while there are many best-of-category restaurants in and around Oklahoma City to prepare a lovely piece of beef, Boulevard Steakhouse will prepare the best steak you'll find in this steak-loving metro—hand-cut, custom aged, and cooked to perfection. (A technicality here: The Boulevard is in Edmond, but if you're in north OKC, that's practically Edmond, too.)

Equally famous for its extensive, all-star wine list, a brilliant cocktail selection, impeccable service, and elegant ambiance (is that Frank Sinatra in the background?) The Boulevard is a can't-miss destination for a romantic dinner, a special occasion, or for impressing a client. Whether you start with the spinach and artichoke dip, the Oysters Rockefeller, or a smooth libation, you'll be well on your way to an exquisite meal. Finish it with Bananas Boulevard!

505 S Blvd., Edmond
(405) 715-2333

21

TAKE THE PARTY OUTSIDE
AT THE BLEU GARTEN

Every Friday, Saturday, and Sunday from March through November, the Bleu Garten in Midtown plays host to families, couples, and friends in a hopping food truck park with all the amenities needed for the ultimate in al fresco dining: shaded seating, live music, lawn games, misters and heaters, full-liquor bars, and the best amenity of all—clean restrooms. Play a game of giant Jenga and be sure to ask someone to snap a photo of you in front of the "Keep Oklahoma Friendly!" mural while you're here.

While the vendors are crowd-vetted as the best in the metro (in 2017, *405 Magazine* readers voted Bleu Garten as OKC's "Best Customer Experience," "Favorite Watering Hole," and "Best Place to Take Visiting Friends/Relatives") the menu from one weekend to the next is as varied as the food trucks that rotate in and out. Check out @BleuGarten on Instagram for the latest updates and specials. Bleu Garten is normally closed December through February, but watch for "flash openings" on social media when winter weather is unseasonably warm!

301 NW 10th St., Oklahoma City
bleugarten.com

22

FILL YOUR TANK
AT THE PUMP BAR

The only thing better than the hip, easy vibe at this Texaco-service-station-turned-bar-and-pub is its fantastic menu of made-to-order drinks and delicious bites from every level of my food pyramid: Okie poutine, bison Frito® chili pie, hot dog sliders, tots, kettle popcorn, and any number of specials from the daily board that will only make your decision harder.

With its spacious (nine thousand square feet) patio and outdoor gaming area, The Pump Bar is inviting almost year-round for a great mix of patrons who flock to the Uptown 23rd neighborhood for concerts at the nearby Tower Theatre or for the convivial nightlife that makes this part of town a date night/girls' night/night out with friends draw. Its menu of sixteen local and specialty beers on tap and more than fifty domestic and import craft bottles is rivaled only by its stellar lineup of whiskey and cocktails, which you can enjoy well into the evening (2:00 a.m.). Trust me, your Uber driver will know how to get here.

2425 N Walker Ave., Oklahoma City
(405) 702-8898
facebook.com/thepumpbar

TASTE THE SOUTHWEST
AT GREEN CHILE KITCHEN ROUTE 66

An important stop on your tour of area culinary favorites will be Green Chile Kitchen Route 66, located about twenty-five minutes west of downtown OKC, on historic Route 66 in Yukon. Green Chile takes its name from this defining ingredient of the Southwest, which is also the fundamental ingredient of almost every made-from-scratch, New Mexican-inspired (not Tex-Mex!) item on the menu. In fact, fresh ingredients elevate the bar on Green Chile's menu, starting with a hat trick of housemade salsas: spicy Tomás salsa, hot habañero salsa, and tomatillo lime salsa.

The posole (chicken soup/stew with New Mexican red chile, hominy, cilantro, onion, lettuce, and corn tortillas) also makes a fine starter, followed by the carne a dovada, similar to a cochinita pibil, with oh-so-tender (sweet) pork that's been slow cooked with red chile spices. Stop by the pie counter on your way out and take home a whole one (think: pie made with a sweet apple and green chile filling, cheddar cheese crust and walnut streusel) for breakfast if you don't have room for dessert.

12 E Main St., Yukon
(405) 265-4346
greenchilekitchen.com

24

A MUST GO:
PIZZERIA GUSTO

The cradle of pizza, as anyone who loves it ought to know, is Naples (Napoli), Italy. For a great pizza, you should start there. But you're not there; you're in Oklahoma City, where the stars have aligned to bring you the next best thing: Pizzeria Gusto, separated at birth from its sisters in Italy and transplanted as OKC's only Neapolitan pizzeria, located in the historic and hip Uptown district near NW 23rd Street.

Everything about this pizza is legit. The purists at Gusto import their tomatoes, flour, and other ingredients from Italy. Even the oven was built by hand in Naples. In the time it takes to cook your made-from-scratch pie (which is about ninety seconds), Gusto will turn you into a pizza snob. (Try not to be annoying about it.) Just see what happens when you taste the honey sriracha on the Gusto pepperoni, the sweetness of the Cherry Tomato, or the hearty Lamb Sausage pizza.

If Pizzeria Gusto suddenly quit making pizza one day, it would still be a destination for its non-pizza menu (roasted red pepper hummus, lamb chops, or gnocchi with braised short ribs, to name a few faves), its Italian wine list, its tap of nearly a dozen beers, and its creative cocktail menu.

2415 N Walker Ave., Oklahoma City
(405) 437-4992
pizzeria-gusto.com

PUT ON YOUR FAT PANTS
FOR THE BUTCHER BBQ STAND

Quite possibly the most decorated (in awards, that is) barbecue restaurant in any part of the country, The Butcher BBQ makes some serious magic happen in the most rustic of ways. Operating from the converted shack of a railcar located thirty minutes from Oklahoma City on Route 66, this stand is only open three days a week—Friday, Saturday, and Sunday—from 11:00 a.m. (get there thirty minutes before that) until the food runs out. You'll dine at a covered outdoor picnic area and there are no restrooms, but you'll gladly trade a few minor annoyances for what you're about to experience—and so will the sixty people in line who are waiting for your table.

Readers of *405 Magazine* call The Butcher BBQ Stand "simply the best BBQ in the 405," but judges at the thirtieth annual Jack Daniels Grand Championship Barbecue event in Lynchburg, Tennessee, (the Super Bowl of BBQ) call The Butcher Team the best in the world, ranking their pork, chicken, ribs, and legendary sauce #1 from a field of 120 competitors. You'll want to try them all (thank me later), adding some "apple pie" baked beans and mac 'n' cheese to the mix. The Butcher keeps dessert uncomplicated: Twinkies are $1. A note on the menu reads, "We are BBQ'ers, not bakers."

3402 W Hwy. 66 (OK 66), Wellston
(405) 240-3437
butcherbbqstand.com

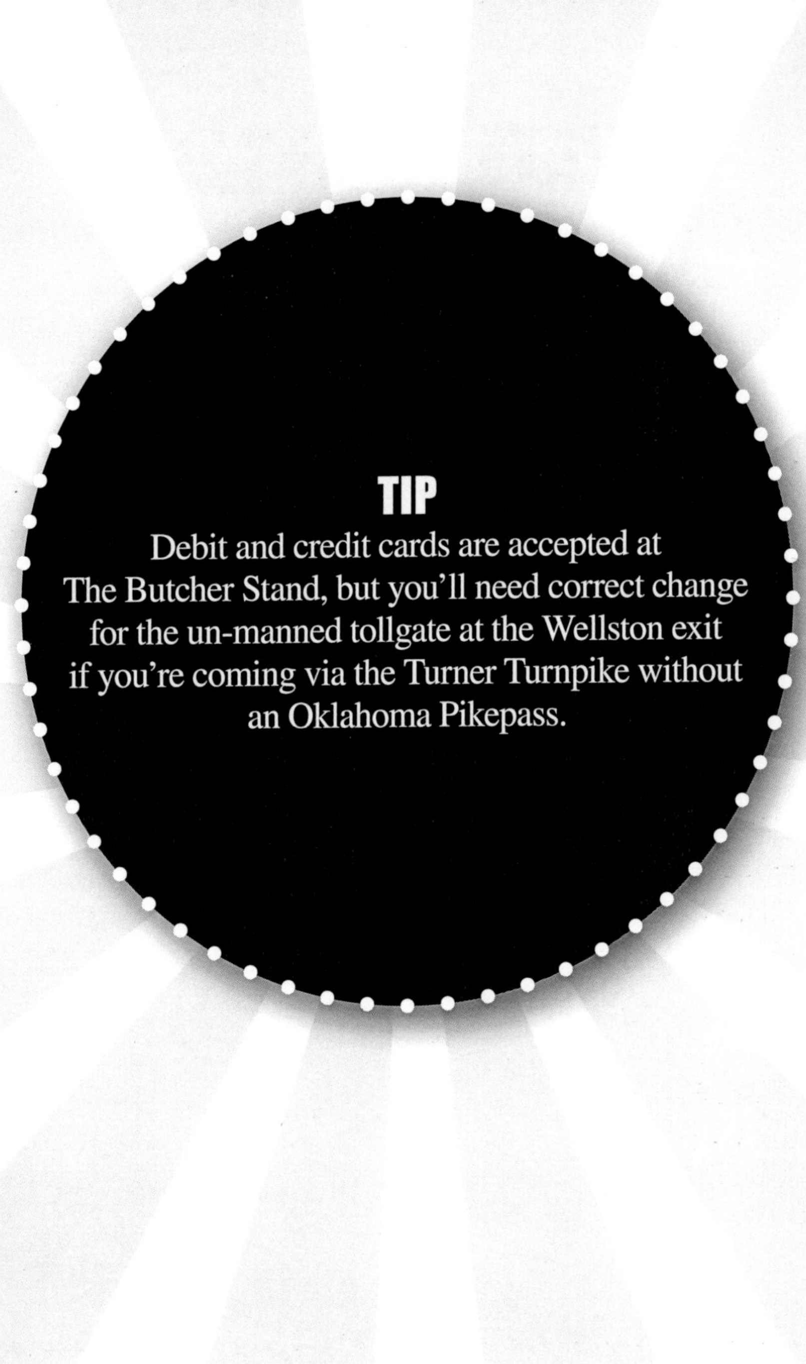

TIP

Debit and credit cards are accepted at The Butcher Stand, but you'll need correct change for the un-manned tollgate at the Wellston exit if you're coming via the Turner Turnpike without an Oklahoma Pikepass.

ELEVATE YOUR TASTE
AT VAST (49TH FLOOR)

Vast takes its name from the sweeping views offered from the top of the Devon Energy Center in Downtown. If rising fifty stories (726.2 feet) above downtown Oklahoma City doesn't put you closer to heaven, Vast's extensive menu of locally sourced steak—dry-aged in-house—should do the trick. For corporate dinners or a big date night, you can't go wrong on any part of Vast's menu, which is subject to change according to seasonal availability of ingredients from local producers, but always carefully curated by renowned OKC chef and restaurateur, Kurt Fleischfresser. Not sure whether to choose the steak or the rack of lamb? Can't decide between the blackened salmon and the grilled tomahawk pork chop? Go off the menu and let Vast's chef create a dining experience that captures the best of the season.

333 W Sheridan Ave., Oklahoma City
(405) 702-7562
vastokc.com

RAISE A GLASS
AT BREWERS UNION

Oklahoma may have been the last to the finish line in the race for modern liquor laws, but persistent voters overwhelmingly emancipated the state from its antiquated beer and liquor restrictions in 2018. Not surprisingly, Oklahoma craft beer has enjoyed a meteoric rise in 2017 and 2018—actually, we've all enjoyed that rise—and local breweries have experienced an industry boom throughout the metro.

Brewing craft beer on a scale that's any larger than your garage is complex and expensive. The Brewers Union at 520 North Meridian Avenue provides a sort of incubation space for startup brewers to get their brands off the ground. In the process, it functions as a taproom that features four different brands for aficionados to sample. Think of it as a mini brew crawl in one spot.

Some of the Brewers Union's fledgling brewers—Angry Scotsman Brewing, Elk Valley Brewing, and Vanessa House Beer Company—have already flown the nest (they grow up so fast!) and are killing it in their own breweries around Oklahoma City, making room for new brewers to incubate at Brewers Union.

See the next two pages for a list of local breweries and taprooms to add to your brew crawl.

520 N Meridian Ave., Oklahoma City
(405) 604-8989
buok.beer

BREW CRAWL

Angry Scotsman Brewing
Brewery, Taproom, Tours, and Beer Garden
with skyline views
704 W Reno Ave., Oklahoma City
(405) 334-7208
angryscotbrew.com

Anthem Brewing Company
Brewery, Growler Station, Tours, Taproom
908 SW 4th St., Oklahoma City
(405) 604-0446
anthembrewing.com

COOP Ale Works
Brewery, Growler Station, Tours, Taproom
4745 Council Heights Rd., Oklahoma City
(405) 842-2667
coopaleworks.com

Elk Valley Brewing Company
1210 N Hudson Ave., Oklahoma City
Brewery, Growler Station, Taproom, Rooftop Bar
(405) 209-0016
elkvalleybrew.com

Prairie Artisan Ales
Brewery, Growler Station, Taproom
3 NE 8th St., Oklahoma City
(405) 602-0894
prairieales.com

Roughtail Brewing Company
Brewery, Growler Station, Tours, Taproom
1279 N Air Depot Blvd., Midwest City*
roughtailbeer.com
* Roughtail expects to relocate in 2019.
Check website for updates.

Stonecloud Brewing Company
Brewery, Growler Station, Tours, Taproom
1012 NW 1st St., Ste. 101, Oklahoma City
(405) 602-3966
stonecloudbrewing.com

Twisted Spike Brewing Company
Brewery, Growler Station, (OKC's largest) Taproom
1 NW 10th St., Oklahoma City
(405) 297-9961
twistedspike.com

Vanessa House Beer Company
Brewery, Growler Station, Tours, Taproom
118 NW 8th St., Oklahoma City
(405) 816-4870
vanessahousebeerco.com

MUSIC AND ENTERTAINMENT

Photo courtesy of Stephen Tyler

28

YOUR TICKET TO CONCERT FUN:

THE TOWER THEATRE

Opened in 1937, the Tower Theatre remains one of a constellation of Oklahoma City's original movie houses with an intact auditorium and neon marquee. The Tower was the undisputed star of the historic Uptown district for decades. Years of neglect eventually caught up with her, and she closed her doors in 1989. In 2017, the Tower reopened after a $6.5 million dollar facelift—triumphantly restored to her former, neon-tastic glory—and instantly emerged as a popular, state-of-the-art concert venue (the acoustics are phenomenal) for regional and national performers.

Check the Tower's website to see who's playing while you're in OKC. Most of the one-thousand-person capacity venue is a standing room, but seating is available if you need it; just call ahead and let the friendly Tower staff know. Park for free in the parking lot across from the Tower's iconic, neon marquee. After the concert, you'll be within steps of some excellent late-night eateries and cozy bars.

425 NW 23rd St., Oklahoma City
(405) 708-6937
towertheatreokc.com

29

GO EARLY, STAY LATE
AT THE JONES ASSEMBLY

The Wallflowers, Willie Nelson, and Andy Grammer walk into a bar . . . If these celebrities are in Oklahoma City, odds are they're walking into The Jones Assembly. Although calling this twenty-thousand-square-foot dream space a "bar" hardly does it justice, this former Ford assembly plant has been "reassembled" into a combination restaurant/bar/concert venue/semi-covered patio/private event space, and Oklahoma City is positively smitten. (Readers of *405 Magazine* named The Jones their 2018 choice for "Best Live Music Venue," "Best Brunch," and "Best Customer Experience," with the T Room taking honors as "Best Cocktail Bar.")

Located on the west end of downtown's historic Film Row, The Jones welcomes national recording artists for live concerts, but the vibe is more of a backyard party highlighted by regional cuisine that touches every culinary base (read: scratch biscuits, wood-fired pizza, steak frites, spicy fried chicken). Its two outdoor patios are perfect spots to settle in for appetizers, cocktails, and conversation. The upstairs T Room has an impressive collection of vinyl LPs, offering a more intimate setting for enjoying a bevvie or four. (If it's spring or summer, start with the refreshing, frozen Frosé.)

901 W Sheridan Ave., Oklahoma City
(405) 212-2378
thejonesassembly.com

CHILL
AT THE JAZZ LAB

I would compare an evening performance at The Jazz Lab to having world-class musicians and performers right in your living room–the setting is that relaxed. This intimate jazz club venue doubles as the home for the renowned Jazz Studies Division of the University of Central Oklahoma (Edmond, Oklahoma) and as a community-focused, live music venue. It's also a regular touring stop for some of the best names in jazz. Most Thursday, Friday, and Saturday nights, you're sure to encounter outstanding live performances of blues, pop, country, bluegrass, or classical music, as well as Broadway-caliber performances. Seating is first come, first served. Food and beverages are available from the neighboring Hideaway Pizza.

100 E 5th St., Edmond
(405) 974-2100
ucojazzlab.com

OKC'S TOP DESTINATION:
BRICKTOWN

Immediately to the east of downtown OKC, Bricktown welcomes locals and visitors to one of the city's liveliest shopping, sports, dining, and entertainment districts. This former warehouse district languished in disrepair as a blighted no-man's land for decades until the early 1990s, when local business owners began to invest in its potential as a vibrant extension of an otherwise sleepy downtown.

If you're staying downtown, you'll be within walking distance to Bricktown, which is now a thriving commercial and entertainment hub with more than 45 restaurants, bars, and retail shops. Family-friendly attractions abound, along with a variety of museums, galleries, and even an urban beach for summer fun. Bricktown is also home to the Chickasaw Bricktown Ballpark and the Oklahoma City Dodgers Triple-A baseball team, the mile-long Bricktown Canal, a 16-screen cineplex, and abundant nightlife venues.

welcometobricktown.com

TIP

To move easily from Bricktown to Midtown and points in between, take a ride on OKC's brand new Streetcar system. Purchase a day pass from your smartphone (download the Token Transit app) or from vending machines at the streetcar platforms for just $3 and you can do a lot of exploring! For holiday and special event schedules, visit okcstreetcar.com.

32

LISTENING ROOM ONLY
AT THE BLUE DOOR

With seating limited to one hundred, the Blue Door brings its listening audience as close to performers as you'll get anywhere. Billed as a "small concert listening room" (the acoustics are spot-on), The Blue Door sets the stage for an intimate exchange between performers and the audience in a casual, neighborhood setting that showcases singer-songwriters like Ellis Paul, Arlo Guthrie, Tracy Grammer, Jimmy Webb, Joe Ely, Ramblin' Jack Elliott, David Lindley, and Tom Rush who cover the gamut of blues, bluegrass, folk, country, and rock.

The Blue Door is a BYOB establishment (wine, beer, and non-alcoholic drinks only) located about three miles north of downtown OKC, so load up your cooler before you head over, and get there early if the performer is well known. (The blue doors on the building will be your cue that you've found the place.) Bonus: there's a cozy outdoor patio with a fire pit for hanging out before and after the show.

2805 N McKinley Ave., Oklahoma City
(405) 524-0738
bluedoorokc.com

TAKE IN A LIVE PERFORMANCE

AT THE CRITERION

The Criterion, nestled in the heart of the Bricktown entertainment district, is quickly becoming Oklahoma City's go-to venue for must-see concerts and events. Since its debut in March of 2016, The Criterion has welcomed national acts, from musicians and comedians to MMA title fights, into a shiny, new, multi-level music hall setting with phenomenal sound and lighting. Even though you can rent out The Criterion for four thousand of your closest friends, this modern gem is often a standing room-only venue.

500 E Sheridan Ave., Oklahoma City
(405) 840-5500
criterionokc.com

WATCH THE STARS
AT AN OUTDOOR SUMMER MOVIE

Summer nights are made for families and summer blockbusters. In Oklahoma City, there's no reason to go indoors for movie night. Every Wednesday night from June through August, bring your picnic (no glass) to enjoy on a blanket or lawn chair on the Great Lawn at the Myriad Gardens in downtown for family-friendly movie fun. The best part? It's free! Movies usually begin at 9:00 p.m., courtesy of Oklahoma City-based Sonic Corporation. Additional food and drinks are available from various food trucks and local vendors.

Equally entertaining is RIVERSPORT Rapids' Floating Films, a free summer movie series on select Fridays from June through September. Watch an outdoor screening of popular family films (projected onto the pump house at the RIVERSPORT Rapids Facility) from the comfort of your blanket or lawn chair (for riverside viewing on the banks of the lower pond) or rent a raft or tube (for guests eight and older) from guest services at the McClendon Whitewater Center and watch from the water while you float! Movies usually begin at 8:30 p.m. Outside food and beverages are not permitted, but you can purchase dinner, snacks, and drinks at the Big Water Grill on the premises.

Sonic Summer Movies at
the Myriad Gardens
301 W Reno Ave., Oklahoma City
(405) 445-7080

RIVERSPORT Floating Films
800 RIVERSPORT Dr.
Oklahoma City
(405) 552-4040

riversportokc.org/events/floating-films

COME FOR THE FUN, STAY FOR THE FOOD

AT THE GREAT STATE FAIR OF OKLAHOMA

Whether you go for the people watching, the rides and attractions, the livestock competitions, concerts and performances, or the food, a visit to the Great State Fair of Oklahoma is the ultimate family-friendly outing—clean, safe, and entertaining.

Every September, more than a million fairgoers come to Oklahoma City to take in all the fair has to offer during eleven action-packed days of entertainment, education, and great food. (I know people who go to the fair every night just to have dinner!) The cinnamon rolls alone are worth the line and the price of admission. You'll never see everything, but the best way to maximize your time here is to come early and stay late.

3001 General Pershing Blvd., Oklahoma City
(405) 948-6700
okstatefair.com

36

YOUR NEIGHBORHOOD HAUNT:
VZD'S

In a former incarnation, VZD's was Veazey Drugstore, complete with a soda fountain and apothecary cases. Locals commonly referred to it as VZD's and the name stuck through the ensuing decades. For the last three decades, VZD's has led a double life as a hip lunch spot by day and even more hip den for live music and cocktails by night, all the while serving as the beating heart of OKC's Western Avenue district. Locally owned and operated, VZD's has long been such an iconic landmark on N Western Avenue that the district has literally grown up around it.

This intimate performance setting is a fantastic live music venue. Local, regional, and national musicians (including the Red Hot Chili Peppers, Bo Diddley, Flaming Lips, Dixie Chicks, and two of my favorites: Brave Combo and A2Z) have rocked it at the VZD.

4200 N Western Ave., Oklahoma City
(405) 602-3006
vzds.com

COUNTRY STARS SHINE
AT THE CENTENNIAL RODEO OPRY THEATER

If it's Saturday night, the Rodeo Opry, Oklahoma's official live country music show, will be hopping in historic Stockyards City. Country music stars Bryan White, Katrina Elam, and Cody Canada of Cross-Canadian Ragweed were once fledgling performers here. Every Saturday night for nearly forty years, the Opry has welcomed musicians, artists, and stars in a high-energy, family-friendly showcase of country and gospel entertainment.

Oklahoma legends Wanda Jackson, Reba McEntire, and Jody Miller are just some of the veteran performers who have returned, not only to perform on the Opry's stage, but to work with rising young local musicians and performers to help open the doors to their future in the music industry. Showtime is 7:00 p.m. (nearly) every Saturday night (except for some holidays).

2221 Exchange Ave., Oklahoma City
(405) 297-9773
ohfo.org

BIG WATER GRILL
BIG WATER GRILL

SPORTS AND RECREATION

SPEND A DAY IN THE SUN
AT THE BOATHOUSE DISTRICT

Water, land, or sky, adventure begins in the Boathouse District, located just south of Bricktown along Lincoln Boulevard, near the intersection of I-35 and I-40. A gateway for outdoor recreation for residents, visitors, and Olympic hopefuls, the Boathouse District is unrivaled in its offerings, comprising architecturally striking boathouses, access to river kayaking, canoeing, tubing, whitewater rafting, a six-story adventure course with a controlled free fall, a zipline that stretches seven hundred feet across the Oklahoma River, a youth zone, and more than thirteen miles of paved trails for running, walking, or cycling for those who prefer to stay on land.

No matter your level of expertise (or passion) for outdoor activity, the Boathouse District is ideal for a day of family fun in the heart of Oklahoma City.

725 S Lincoln Blvd., Oklahoma City
riversportokc.org

GO TO EXTREMES
AT THE EXTREME WATER SLIDES

For outstanding water fun, it's hard to beat the Extreme Water Slides in the Boathouse District!

Slather on your SPF 45 and start at the Hippo Slide, a forty-four-foot-tall water slide that will send you down 175 feet of slippery water duct in a hurry. Ready to add some air? Go airborne and prepare for a splash-landing on Big Air—another forty-four-footer that will launch you skyward then down into the inflatable landing zone below.

New in 2019, Slide the Rapids starts as a forty-foot-tall water slide and turns into a six-hundred-foot Slip 'n' Slide that will give you a wild hurtle down to Love's Island.

Extreme slides have a maximum weight requirement of 250 pounds and a minimum height requirement of forty-eight inches.

800 RIVERSPORT Dr., Oklahoma City
(405) 552-4040
riversportokc.org

FUN-ONLY ZONE
AT RIVERSPORT OKC'S YOUTH ZONE

Family fun comes in all sizes at RIVERSPORT OKC's Youth Zone. Here are some highlights for maximizing your vacation experience:

A junior-sized adventure course, Sky Tykes, is a smaller version of the SandRidge Sky Trail. Parents can accompany their child(ren) (maximum height for kids is forty-eight inches) through exciting challenges just a few feet off the ground.

Kick off your shoes and hop on a cloud! The Cloud Bounce is a forty-eight-foot inflatable pillow that takes jumping to a whole new level.

When you're ready for some more sky adventure, take a ride on the Kids Zip, a miniature zipline, or try some jumps and flips twenty feet in the air, bungee-style, on the Extreme Air Jumper.

For land lovers, there's plenty of fun on the playground, too!

800 RIVERSPORT Dr., Oklahoma City
(405) 552-4040
riversportokc.org

BLAZE YOUR OWN TRAIL
ON THE SANDRIDGE SKY TRAIL

The eighty-foot SandRidge Sky Trail has been called a "playground in the sky." The tallest adventure course of its kind in the world, the Sky Trail is a seven-story vertical ropes course that challenges climbers at each level, becoming increasingly difficult as you climb higher. Rope bridges, balance beams, and other obstacles must be overcome on your way up. Once you've conquered those challenges and reached the top, you'll have some adrenaline-inducing options for your return to the ground: an eighty-foot free fall called the Rumble Drop or the high-speed, seventy-two-foot Sky Slide. If you'd prefer a more low-key descent, you can always take the stairs back down.

800 RIVERSPORT Dr., Oklahoma City
(405) 552-4040
riversportokc.org

FALL
FOR THE RUMBLE DROP

Have you ever wondered what it would feel like to skydive? The Rumble Drop is an exhilarating (controlled) free-fall experience, just one option to take you down from the top of the SandRidge SkyTrail—the only catch, of course, is that you must first make your way up the eighty-foot structure, whether through the vertical ropes course or up several flights of stairs.

You'll be safely secured with a safety cable that will slow your descent, but it won't slow the adrenaline rush that comes with free falling eighty feet! The Rumble Drop relies on PowerFan technology that provides all the feels as you drop, but without the bounce you'd experience by bungee jumping, for example. Either way, you're sure to find your stomach in your throat at the bottom.

800 RIVERSPORT Dr., Oklahoma City
(405) 552-4040
riversportokc.org

TAKE IT FROM THE TOP
ON THE SANDRIDGE SKY ZIP!

Starting from the top of the eighty-foot tall SandRidge Sky Trail, enjoy a fantastic view of the OKC skyline as you take flight seven hundred feet across the Oklahoma River on the SandRidge Sky Zip. Your return trip is an equally exhilarating seven hundred feet back, traveling about 12-15 mph through the sky to the north shore.

You'll need protective footwear, of course—no flip flops or sandals without a back strap—and you'll have to empty your pockets before you're harnessed in. Come early and reserve your zip time—zips are popular and sell out early on busy days.

800 RIVERSPORT Dr., Oklahoma City
(405) 552-4040
riversportokc.org

MAKE WAVES
AT RIVERSPORT RAPIDS

Feeling adventurous? Whether you're whitewater rafting, kayaking, canoeing, or tubing your way through this state-of-the-art facility, you're sure to enjoy an exhilarating water adventure at RIVERSPORT Rapids. More than a million gallons of water per minute power two challenging whitewater courses, guaranteed to move you downstream in a hurry! Even first-timers will enjoy learning to navigate the course with the help of RIVERSPORT's trained guides who provide all the safety and technical instruction necessary to ensure a safe journey. Your guide will also accompany you. A rafting session will last about ninety minutes and you'll be required to wear a life jacket and helmet (provided by the center). If you want to take things a little slower, choose the tubing option. Kids must be at least eight years old to participate.

800 RIVERSPORT Dr., Oklahoma City
(405) 552-4040
riversportokc.org

BANK ON FUN
AT THE OKLAHOMA REGATTA FESTIVAL

Late September is a beautiful time of year in OKC, which means the weather will almost certainly be perfect for the Oklahoma Regatta Festival, a three-day, family-friendly celebration of rowing, kayaking, whitewater raft racing, and dragon boating competitions in the Boathouse District.

Bring your lawn chair or picnic blanket and cheer on racing teams from around the US as they compete in the Oklahoma City University "Head of the Oklahoma" race, a two-and-a-half-mile course that features college, masters, and junior rowing. Each evening, the OG&E NightSprints race, a five-hundred-meter competition that takes place at sunset, features dragon boat races and rowing races.

Food trucks and beer gardens abound, so settle in and enjoy the fireworks later in the evening. Admission is free; parking is $10.

725 S Lincoln Blvd., Oklahoma City
riversportokc.org/events/oklahoma-regatta-festival

TAKE A SUNSET SPIN
AT WHEELER PARK

In 2008, local businessman Grant Humphreys was the winning bidder for an unusual eBay catch: the Santa Monica Pier Ferris wheel. Following the wheel's relocation to OKC (it's unlikely that the eBay purchase included free shipping), it underwent a million-dollar renovation and quickly became an iconic representation of the city's unbridled growth and enthusiasm for bringing community together.

An ideal time to take the wheel for a spin is during a spectacular sunset over neighboring downtown and the Boathouse District. The sweeping view is fabulous! Once you're back on terra firma, visit a nearby food truck and have a picnic along the Wheeler Riverfront Plaza, or just kick back in a hammock and watch the world go by. Rides are $6 per person and you'll find plenty of free parking close by. Open April through November.

1701 S Western Ave., Oklahoma City
(405) 655-8455
wheelerdistrict.com/ferris-wheel

47

TAKE SIDES

FOR OU/OSU BEDLAM

The fan rivalry between the University of Oklahoma Sooners and Oklahoma State University Cowboys runs deep and long. They call it "Bedlam," which might be an understatement, given the ferocity of the rivalry and the fact that conference championships are often on the line when it comes to games between these rivals. Attending a sporting event for either side is a quintessential Oklahoman experience, and both universities are a relatively short drive from Oklahoma City. When the schools face off against one another, brace yourself and take a side. There's no room for neutrality where Bedlam is concerned!

For athletics schedules, go online:
University of Oklahoma (Norman): soonersports.com
Oklahoma State University (Stillwater): okstate.com

GO WILD
AT THE OKLAHOMA CITY ZOO AND BOTANICAL GARDEN

Oklahoma's number one cultural attraction is home to more than two thousand animals on more than one hundred acres amid beautifully appointed botanical gardens, the Oklahoma City Zoo connects more than one million visitors each year to wildlife in its state-of-the-art habitats, including the Great EscApe, Cat Forest/ Lion Overlook, Oklahoma Trails Adventure, the Children's Zoo, and the recently opened Sanctuary Asia, a 6.6-acre habitat for endangered animals from the Asian continent.

For a one-of-a-kind experience, go behind the scenes with Wild Encounters for a closer look at grizzly bears, flamingos, elephants, rhinos, sea lions, or Galapagos tortoises. (Additional cost applies.)

No matter when you're in town, there's always something happening at the zoo!

2101 NE 50th Street, Oklahoma City
(405) 424-3344
okczoo.org

TIP

Children under age three are admitted free of charge. Parking is free and same day re-entry is allowed. The zoo also offers a 50 percent discount on general admission to all veterans, active duty, active reserves, and retirees of the military (with valid military ID). Discount does not apply to children or dependents of veterans, active duty, active reserves, or retirees of the military.

Also—the Zoo Amphitheater has a number of great outside musical performances during the summer.

TAKE ME OUT
TO THE OKC DODGERS GAME

Professional baseball came to Oklahoma City in 1904 and the state has never stopped cheering. The cheers grew louder in 2014, when the organization became the Oklahoma City Dodgers, the AAA affiliate to the LA Dodgers.

The Chickasaw Bricktown Ballpark ("the Brick") is home to the Dodgers and to thousands of baseball-loving fans who devote the better part of spring and summer to America's favorite pastime in this fantastic venue.

On your way into the Brick, you'll cross through one (or all) of three plazas, dedicated to Oklahoma baseball greats: native sons Mickey Mantle and Johnny Bench, and "the greatest lefty of all time," former Oklahoma resident Warren Spahn.

Dodgers games are family outings—kids will never be bored (or hungry!). Players interact with fans before the game. Several activities for kids are planned between innings. If you go on a Friday night, stay for the fireworks after the game and don't miss the Dodgers' team store, located along Mickey Mantle Drive on the west side of the ballpark, for souvenirs, hats and apparel, specialty gear, and collectibles.

Chickasaw Bricktown Ballpark
2 S Mickey Mantle Dr., Oklahoma City
(405) 218-1000
milb.com/oklahoma-city

50

HOW THE WEST WAS FUN:
FRONTIER CITY

Oklahoma's largest theme park is the ultimate family destination for play. Frontier City celebrates the Wild West with thirty rides and attractions across its forty-acre park, including five roller coasters, a well-developed collection of water rides, and a children's play area (with a petting zoo). The park also doubles as a concert venue in its open-air Starlight Amphitheater, home to the free Summer Concert Series (concert admission is free with park admission purchase).

Frontier City is open April to November, with special seasonal openings around certain holidays. FrightFest makes Frontier City one of OKC's favorite "haunts" every October, featuring the largest and scariest haunted house in the city. New in 2018, Frontier City's "Holiday in the Park" is a total park transformation to a holiday winter wonderland. From late November through early January, the park is aglow with more than a million colorful lights, while popular rides and attractions are re-opened for thrilling holiday entertainment.

In 2019, Frontier City will debut a new children's area called Timber Town, featuring four new attractions for pint-sized thrill seekers, including a new family coaster called Frankie's Mine Train, billed as being "as wild as the West itself."

11501 N I-35 Service Rd., Oklahoma City
(405) 478-2140
frontiercity.com

GET LOUD
WITH THE OKLAHOMA CITY THUNDER

Ever since the Thunder rumbled into town in 2008, they have never looked back: our big league city continues to sell out every home game. At the newly renovated Chesapeake Arena, OKC's favorite NBA team thrills crowds about forty-two times per year.

No matter where you sit, you might think about using some earplugs in this high-energy (and even higher decibel) crowd. Thunder fans are an "arrive early and stay late" crowd that emanates all the energy of the final seconds of an NBA Finals game—no matter the game, no matter the score. While nearby options abound for pre-game dinner and drinks, the entertainment and food inside the arena are first-class, rivaling any other downtown restaurant.

Head up to "Love's Loud City" balcony and mezzanine sections and find out how OKC earned its title as "the loudest city in the NBA." These aren't nosebleed seats with unengaged fans. You will find the same quality of fan and food with an amazing view of the game.

Chesapeake Energy Arena
100 W Reno Ave., Oklahoma City
(405) 208-4800
nba.com/thunder

52

PLAY ALL DAY AND NIGHT
AT BRICKOPOLIS

Directly across from the Chickasaw Bricktown Ballpark, Brickopolis offers fun for the entire family in a three-level entertainment megaplex with laser tag, miniature golf, arcade games, and gemstone mining.

The third floor is home to more than thirty arcade games, a laser tag arena, and sweeping views of Bricktown from above. The second floor (street level) offers the Brickopolis Bar and Grill, an ideal place for adults to relax on the patio and enjoy a burger, full bar service, and the best people-watching on the Bricktown Canal. The family-friendly canal level includes a buffet, a fully stocked salad bar, pizza, and children's games.

When the weather is nice, put your putting skills to the test on the challenging eighteen-hole miniature golf course. Complete with cascading waterfalls and fountains, this mini course will test even the best of putt-putters with some really tricky holes!

101 S Mickey Mantle Dr., Oklahoma City (Bricktown)
(405) 516-2745
brickopolisu.com

53

VISIT A DOWNTOWN OASIS

AT MYRIAD BOTANICAL GARDENS AND CRYSTAL BRIDGE CONSERVATORY

In the heart of Downtown, the Myriad Botanical Gardens are an urban retreat, spanning seventeen multi-tiered, landscaped acres. Ornamental gardens, a children's garden and playground, a dog park, and a band shell overlooking the Great Lawn are just a few of the features in this natural oasis that the *Minneapolis Star Tribune* recently named as a top 10 public park.

Activities take place in the gardens virtually year-round. In spring, summer, or fall, you're likely to catch free live concerts on the Great Lawn. From mid-November through early February, lace up your skates and practice your axel at the open-air Devon Ice Rink, open seven days a week at the northeast corner of the gardens.

The crown jewel of the gardens is the Crystal Bridge Conservatory, a thirteen-thousand-square-foot living plant museum featuring thousands of tropical and desert plants, palm trees, a thirty-five-foot waterfall, and spectacular panoramic views from a skywalk across the center of the conservatory.

301 W Reno Ave., Oklahoma City
(405) 445-7080
oklahomacitybotanicalgardens.com

GET ON YOUR MARKS
AT THE REDBUD CLASSIC

Every spring, more than two hundred thousand athletes and wannabes take to the streets, either in running shoes or on bicycles, for the annual Redbud Classic, an Oklahoma City tradition for nearly forty years. This race, part competition and part philanthropic event, supports local nonprofit organizations by bringing the community together every April.

No matter your age or fitness level, the Redbud Classic has many opportunities for participation, including bike tours of ten, thirty-three, and forty-five miles, a one-mile kids' fun run, 5k and 10k runs, a 5k wheelchair event, a two-mile walk, and a baby stroller derby.

The beneficiary of the run changes from year to year. Start and finish lines are located at the Waterford Complex Building at NW 63rd Street and Pennsylvania Avenue.

NW 63rd St. and Pennsylvania Ave.
(405) 842-8295
redbud.org

DEFY GRAVITY

AT IFLY OKC INDOOR SKYDIVING

Feel the amazing sensation of indoor skydiving at iFly OKC. Your adventure begins with the assistance of a trained flight instructor, who will help you with proper body positioning and other techniques. The folks at iFly will provide your helmet, flight suit, and goggles. Once you've suited up, it's time to fly! Your instructor will accompany you inside the flight chamber where the wind tunnel will lift you to new heights!

From start to finish, your iFly experience will last about one and a half to two hours. Everyone is required to sign a waiver before participating to protect the company in case of injury. Flyers under age 18 must have a waiver completed and signed by a parent or guardian prior to gearing up. Once that is done, get ready to fly!

13600 Pawnee Dr., Oklahoma City
(405) 300-4359
iflyworld.com/oklahoma-city

DOWNTOWN IN DECEMBER:

31 DAYS OF MERRIMENT

December is especially festive because of events like Downtown in December. For the entire month, Oklahoma City hosts winter fun for everyone. Most events are free of charge.

Lace up your skates and take to the ice on the Devon Ice Rink at the Myriad Botanical Gardens, one of the most popular attractions during the months of November, December, and January. Hop aboard the Bricktown Water Taxi for a free ride down the canal to see the sparkling holiday decorations (a round-trip tour takes about twenty to thirty minutes). For more lights, head a few blocks north of downtown to Automobile Alley (on Broadway Avenue, from NW 4th to NW 10th Streets) and see the magic that comes when more than 180,000 holiday LED lights illuminate eight city blocks. Finally, knock out all your holiday shopping at the Holiday Pop-Up Shops in Midtown (at NW 10th and Hudson, next to Bleu Garten), open Thursday through Sunday in December.

Various locations in and around downtown OKC
(405) 235-3500
downtownindecember.com

BE A PART OF THE SKYLINE
ON THE SKYDANCE PEDESTRIAN BRIDGE

Beauty, form, and function converge in the iconic Skydance Pedestrian Bridge, giving pedestrians a stunning view of the downtown OKC skyline and a safe means to cross over ten lanes of the heavily-traveled Interstate 40 below. The bridge was designed to connect downtown to the north and south sections of the brand new Scissortail Park, which is scheduled to open in June 2019 (north section), and again in 2021 (south section).

The bridge's design is inspired by the "sky dance" of Oklahoma's state bird, the scissor-tailed flycatcher. Soaring 185 feet high, its "wings" sparkle by day, stretching 440 feet across the interstate. By nightfall, the bridge changes colors to illuminate a portion of Interstate 40 and the night skies above.

Bring your camera to capture the view! Access the bridge at the Western Avenue exit off I-40 (you'll find metered street parking nearby at SW 7th Street and Harvey Avenue) or at the Robinson/Shields Avenue exit off I-40 (you'll also find street parking nearby at SW 10th Street and Harvey Avenue).

I-40, near the Robinson/Shields Avenue Exit, Oklahoma City
(405) 297-8912

DISCOVER
THE BRAND NEW SCISSORTAIL PARK

Billed as a seventy-acre urban oasis on the Oklahoma City website, Scissortail Park is a core-to-shore project (extending from the "core" of downtown Oklahoma City to the "shore" of the Oklahoma River) that is unprecedented in this market. This large central park (which was named through a social media contest) straddles the north and south sides of Interstate 40, connected via the Skydance Pedestrian Bridge.

The north (upper) section of the park is scheduled to open in June 2019. Its features include a 3.7-acre lake with a boathouse, a 240-foot pedestrian bridge that spans the lake, a six-acre oval lawn with a bandshell, an enclosed dog park, a large playground area, a promenade, café and concession areas, and a picnic grove among the park's ornamental gardens and woodlands.

The south (lower) section of the park will open in 2021, bringing an event space, a grassed amphitheater, and a community garden. Designed to be a popular destination for concerts, festivals, and outdoor recreation of all kinds, Scissortail Park promises to offer something for the whole family!

I-40, between S Hudson and S Robinson Avenues, Oklahoma City
scissortailpark.org

59

EXPLORE BRICKTOWN
BY WATER TAXI

Hop aboard a Bricktown Water Taxi to learn a little history and to enjoy a relaxing tour of the city's favorite entertainment district. This experience is sure to be a highlight of your Bricktown visit as your charming Water Taxi Ambassador gives you a "behind the scenes" account of Bricktown, Oklahoma City, and all the points of interest along this scenic ride through the Bricktown Canal. The full ride lasts about forty minutes, although your purchased ticket is valid all day, so hop on and off as many times as you like while you explore Bricktown's many restaurants, shops, sites, and events.

Buy tickets at the ticket booth (111 S Mickey Mantle Drive, next to Brickopolis) or purchase tickets with your smartphone. Regular service departs every fifteen to twenty minutes from the main dock, located just below the ticket booth. From November through April, the availability of service depends on the weather, but if it's nice outside, you'll probably catch a ride!

111 S Mickey Mantle Dr., Oklahoma City (Bricktown)
(405) 234-8294
bricktownwatertaxi.com

TIP

During certain evenings throughout November and December, holiday-themed Water Taxi Rides are free for all ages to enjoy the festive, sparkling Bricktown Canal in all its holiday splendor. Board at the main dock and enjoy the 20- to 30-minute ride.

60

MEET HOMETOWN HEROES

AT THE OKLAHOMA SPORTS HALL OF FAME AND JIM THORPE MUSEUM

Some of the most famous world athletes hail from Oklahoma. Come see the mementos of some of their historic athletic accomplishments—from Heisman trophies to Super Bowl rings, Olympic memorabilia to national awards—in the newly relocated Oklahoma Sports Hall of Fame in the upper northwest corner of the Chickasaw Bricktown Ballpark.

Through a new partnership with the OKC Dodgers baseball organization, the Hall of Fame relocated in April 2018 to its new, thirteen-thousand-square-foot facility that overlooks left field, providing free, convenient access for Dodgers fans and Bricktown visitors to tour this collective celebration of home-state athletes who triumphed at regional, national, and international levels. The sheer volume of memorabilia allows the museum to rotate exhibits about every three to six months, so there's usually something new to see. Open Tuesday through Saturday, 10:00 a.m. to 5:00 p.m. Admission is free.

(Inside the Chickasaw Bricktown Ballpark)
20 S Mickey Mantle Dr., Oklahoma City
(405) 427-1400
oklahomasportshalloffame.org

REACH THE SUMMIT AT THE SILOS:

SUMMIT OKC

Ever wonder what it would be like to climb a commercial grain silo? Once the tallest buildings in the city, these grain silos were converted to a climbing gym in 1999. While ownership has changed hands over the years, the mission to provide a stellar climbing experience hasn't.

Notice the breathtaking mural on the exterior of the silos by local artist Rick Sinnett, titled *This Land*. The cool part? There are routes to climb right up the mural. Your reward will be some amazing views of the Oklahoma City skyline.

Inside, routes are climate-controlled, with multiple opportunities for top rope, lead, auto-belay, and bouldering. Everyone must complete a waiver before their climb. It's available online, so you can save time by filling it out before you arrive. If you're new to climbing, your experience will begin with a facilities introduction and tour which will show you "the ropes."

Climbing experience not enough? Try their newly added yoga studio to get in a good stretch before and after your climb.

200 SE 4th St., Oklahoma City
(405) 673-7448
summitgyms.com/okc-silos

62

VISIT THE SOFTBALL CAPITAL OF THE WORLD:

USA NATIONAL SOFTBALL HALL OF FAME COMPLEX AND MUSEUM

As the home of the National Softball Hall of Fame, the NCAA Women's College World Series, and arguably the finest softball facility in the sport, Oklahoma City is the softball capital of the world!

If you're here in May, the tickets to score are for the NCAA Women's College World Series, a national championship series that attracts nearly eighty thousand fans every year.

The complex is also the home of the annual World Cup of Softball, a competition among the top five teams in the world.

Adjacent to the stadium, the National Softball Hall of Fame is a meticulously curated collection of photos and memorabilia that tell the story of softball's beginnings and its evolution as one of America's favorite sports. Don't miss the gift shop during your visit for T-shirts and apparel, books, gifts, and training videos.

2801 NE 50th St., Oklahoma City
(405) 424-5266
teamusa.org/usa-softball/about/national-softball-hall-of-fame

SEE THE GOLD RUSH
AT THE US OLYMPIC AND PARALYMPIC TRAINING SITE

Watch world-class athletes train in the Boathouse District as they prepare for the 2020 Summer Olympic Games in Tokyo. Receiving the rare designation as a US Olympic and Paralympic Training Site by the US Olympic Committee (USOC), the Boathouse District features elite training facilities for whitewater and flatwater canoeing/kayaking and rowing.

If you're ready to get in on the fun, you don't have to be an Olympic hopeful to participate. RIVERSPORT School offers lessons in rowing, sailing, and flatwater kayaking for individuals who are eight years old and older. For ages ten and older, RIVERSPORT school teaches whitewater kayaking basics in a ninety-minute class. You can even arrange for private lessons if you'd prefer more individualized instruction.

800 RIVERSPORT Dr., Oklahoma City
(405) 552-4040
riversport.org/lessons

CHEER ON
OKC ENERGY FC'S "BOYS IN GREEN"

When professional soccer came to Oklahoma City in 2014, it came in a big way: the fan base was instantaneous and the team was named Rookie Franchise of the Year for the United Soccer League.

The home turf for OKC Energy FC is the historic and recently renovated Taft Stadium, where thousands of futbol-loving fans routinely cheer the "boys in green" through the regular season (March through October) and into the playoffs. While the hyper-spirited "fan zone" supporters can get pretty raucous at games, this is largely a family event, with plenty of activities to keep your kids entertained.

To keep the adults entertained (if the action on the field isn't enough), the COOP Ale Works Beer Garden offers brews with a view.

The stadium is located at NW 27th and May Avenue. Parking is available directly east of the stadium or just to the northeast at Northwest Classen High School.

Taft Stadium, 2501 N May Ave., Oklahoma City
(405) 235-5425
energyfc.com

65

RECONNECT WITH NATURE
AT MARTIN PARK

Tucked away along the Memorial Corridor, a leading retail and medical area, Martin Park (formerly called Martin Park Nature Center) is a secluded escape from the city. This wildlife sanctuary and park, stretching across 140 acres of forest, grasslands, and rocky streams, is an ideal setting for nature exploration, hiking, and interactive learning.

During guided hikes along 2.5 miles of woodland trails or while overlooking the park's twenty-acre pond, you're bound to encounter an abundance of wildlife in this natural setting–white-tailed deer, owls, raccoons, foxes, coyotes, beavers, and native birds of every variety live in this wooded oasis. The park's newly renovated education center reopened in 2018, offering classes, activities, and camps for adults and children. The park also features a nature-themed playground. Open Wednesdays through Sundays, 9:00 a.m. to 6:00 p.m. It is closed each year on city holidays, Thanksgiving, Christmas, New Year's Eve, and New Year's Day. See okc.gov for exact holiday closing days.

5000 W Memorial Rd., Oklahoma City
(405) 297-1429
okc.gov/recreation/martin-nature-park

CULTURE AND HISTORY

BE A PIONEER
AT THE HARN HOMESTEAD

Step back in time to the turn of the nineteenth century and experience early pioneer life as it was in Oklahoma Territory. This well-preserved Victorian farmhouse, located in the heart of the city, was once the home of the William Fremont Harn family. Land disputes were common after the territory's 1889 Land Run. Harn received an appointment from President Benjamin Harrison in 1891 to settle disputes on behalf of the federal government. The homestead is now a private museum that features an 1897 one-room schoolhouse, a 1904 barn, immaculate gardens, and other remnants of a territorial farm.

With many hands-on activities for kids, such as grinding corn, mucking the stalls in the barn, and making rope, they're sure to remember their pioneer experience for years to come.

1721 N Lincoln Blvd., Oklahoma City
(405) 235-4058
harnhomestead.com

SCREEN THEM ALL
AT deadCENTER FILM FESTIVAL

Oklahoma's largest film festival (so named for Oklahoma City's geographical position in the "dead center" of the United States) takes place every June and features four days of independent films from around the world. More than thirty thousand attendees enjoy screenings of well over one hundred films of various genres—comedies, short films, documentaries, animation, and horror flicks among them—attracting budding talent and established film veterans alike. *MovieMaker* magazine calls deadCENTER one of the "Top 20 Coolest Film Festivals in the World," listing it among its "Top Festivals Worth the Entry Fee."

Why should you attend? It's a great chance to see exciting new short films, insightful documentaries, hilarious comedies, scary monster movies, and the best independent films from around the world and all over Oklahoma. Plus, you might just see a movie star or two.

Screening locations vary; check website for details.
(405) 246-9233
deadcenterfilm.org

OKC'S RITE OF SPRING:
FESTIVAL OF THE ARTS

An undisputed rite of spring is the Festival of the Arts, a six-day celebration of creativity, presented by Arts Council OKC. For more than fifty years, this perennial showcase of talent by about twelve dozen presenters (selected from a pool of about 450 applicants nationwide) has attracted visitors from all over the US; nearly three quarters of a million people attend the festival each year. In addition to a spectacular assembly of visual art, including glass blowing and pottery demonstrations, the festival features hour-by-hour entertainment of every variety on several stages throughout downtown's Bicentennial Park. Culinary arts receive top billing, as well, with more than thirty food vendors who bring the best of the best to share with hungry art aficionados. You'll find the longest lines at the Indian Tacos and the Strawberries Newport tents, but they're worth twice the wait.

The Festival of the Arts takes place the last week of April, rain or shine, Tuesday through Saturday, 11:00 a.m. until 9:00 p.m., and Sunday, 11:00 a.m. until 6:00 p.m.

Bicentennial Park (downtown between Lee Ave. and Walker Ave., and Colcord Ave. and Couch Dr.)
artscouncilokc.com

- There are several parking options available near the Festival of the Arts. Check parkingokc.com for a listing.
- Bring the pups! Four-legged art lovers are welcome (and subject to a lot of friendly attention).
- There will be plenty of portable toilets available, but they're the really nice kind, so don't worry if you have to go!

REFLECT AND REMEMBER

AT THE OKLAHOMA CITY NATIONAL MEMORIAL AND MUSEUM

Any visit to the city must include a couple of hours at the Oklahoma City National Memorial and Museum, which honors the victims and survivors of the April 19, 1995, bombing of the Alfred P. Murrah Federal Building that claimed 168 lives. The iconic "Gates of Time" (9:01 a.m. and 9:03 a.m.) stand as bookends on either end of a 318-foot reflecting pool. Nearby, the Memorial's "Survivor Tree," an American Elm that withstood the same blast that decimated dozens of nearby buildings, stands as a reminder of life after tragedy. The Survivor Tree overlooks 168 bronze and glass chairs, each representing a life lost in the blast.

Inside the museum, visitors experience Oklahoma City as it was during the moments just prior to the bombing, before hearing the explosion, and throughout the confusion and chaos that ensued. A $10 million renovation to the museum brought with it several hands-on, interactive features that tell more about the story of the bombing, the rescue efforts, the evidence left behind (including convicted terrorist Timothy McVeigh's getaway car), the investigation, and the aftermath.

620 N Harvey Avenue
(405) 235-3313
oklahomacitynationalmemorial.org

SIDE NOTE

Many people believe that Oklahoma City changed in the aftermath of the April 19, 1995 bombing. Amid the chaos that morning, people responded with every imaginable act of goodwill. Then and now, Oklahomans wouldn't think twice about offering help or support to total strangers. In 1995, non-local observers called it "the Oklahoma Standard," an expression that's widely used today in reference to the compassion and kindness often attributed to Oklahomans.

TIP

The Memorial Mobile App provides general information, video and audio tours, and interactive content for the Memorial. Search OKCNM in the Apple App Store or in Google Play and download the guides for free.

70

MARVEL AT CHIHULY'S MAGIC

AT THE OKLAHOMA CITY MUSEUM OF ART (OKCMOA)

Located in the heart of downtown, the Oklahoma City Museum of Art is a must-see for natives and visitors alike, representing five centuries of artistic highlights, European and American masterpieces, and works by Georgia O'Keeffe and Dale Chihuly.

You'll be in awe of the OKCMOA's signature sculpture at the museum's entrance, the Eleanor Blake Kirkpatrick Memorial Tower, a fifty-five-foot glass sculpture created by renowned glass artist, Dale Chihuly, assembled from 2,400 hand-blown pieces of glass. Many other Chihuly pieces are on permanent display in the OKCMOA, which is home to one of the largest Chihuly collections in the world, a magical installment named Dale Chihuly: Magic & Light.

The museum also features European and American art from the nineteenth through twenty-first centuries, in addition to contemporary art and a variety of special exhibitions throughout the year.

On Fridays and Saturdays, OKCMOA is also home to special gallery programs for babies (Babies at the Museum, for babies up to twenty-four months) and toddlers (Museum Playdate, for children ages two to four years). Reservations are required. Check the website for session dates and titles.

After your visit, stop by for lunch or dinner at the Museum Café, an outstanding full-service restaurant and bar.

Closed Mondays and Tuesdays.

415 Couch Dr., Oklahoma City
(405) 236-3100
okcmoa.com

TOUR
THE OKLAHOMA STATE CAPITOL

Constructed in 1917, the Oklahoma State Capitol is a beautiful example of Greco-Roman architecture, situated amid a complex of one hundred acres and adorned with hand-painted ceilings, stained glass windows, portraits of famous Oklahomans, changing art exhibits, and—perhaps most notably—a working oil derrick on the Capitol's front lawn.

Admission to the Capitol is free. The Oklahoma Department of Tourism and Recreation conducts daily tours for visitors that can be scheduled in advance (Monday through Friday from 9:00 a.m. until 3:00 p.m.; allow about forty-five minutes), or take your time with a self-guided tour. Guided tours begin at the Welcome Center in the first-floor rotunda.

Be sure to see the Oklahoma Veterans Memorial, located on the north side of the Capitol complex, which honors those who fought in World War I, World War II, and the Korean and Vietnam wars, as depicted on the memorial's four walls.

2300 N Lincoln Blvd., Oklahoma City
(405) 521-3356

GO BACK TO THE BEGINNING
AT THE OKLAHOMA HISTORY CENTER

For a comprehensive look at the state's origins, the Oklahoma History Center, located across from the Oklahoma State Capitol, gives visitors a fascinating ride through time with artifacts, photographs, and displays throughout five galleries in this bright, airy 215,000 square-foot museum.

More than two thousand artifacts depict Oklahoma's past, beginning with the replica of Wiley Post's world-famous Winnie Mae airplane, a seven-passenger Lockheed Vega that Post flew around the world in a record-setting eight days in 1931. The Winnie Mae replica is suspended in air in the rotunda of the Devon Great Hall, which also offers a fantastic view of the state capitol and downtown OKC.

The first Saturday of the month is Hands-on History, featuring special family activities throughout the museum, and there is free admission for active military personnel and children under age five. The museum is closed on Sundays.

800 Nazih Zuhdi Dr., Oklahoma City
(405) 522-0765
okhistory.org/historycenter

73

BONE UP ON ANATOMY
AT THE MUSEUM OF OSTEOLOGY

More than three hundred complete skeletons await at Oklahoma City's bone headquarters, the Museum of Osteology, located about fifteen minutes south of Downtown.

This privately owned museum features a fascinating collection of animal bones. Throughout different sections of the museum, visitors can participate in hands-on activities including handling real animal skulls. Check out one of the biggest skeletons on display, a humpback whale, measuring about forty feet in length. Discover how animals like penguins, gophers, sloths, and monkeys have adapted to suit their changing environments.

Learn about the distinguishing characteristics of various species, then test yourself on the Mystery Skulls challenge. Take a closer look at forensic pathology and see how evidence on skulls can hint at the cause of death.

If you still can't get enough bones, be sure to stop in the Skulls Unlimited shop next door, where you'll find rare, real bones or replica items for purchase.

Open daily, with limited hours on Sundays.

10301 S Sunnylane Rd., Oklahoma City
(405) 814-0006
museumofosteology.org

SEE AND BE SEEN
IN THE PASEO ARTS DISTRICT

A colorful, eclectic collection of art galleries, studios, shops, restaurants, and cafés, the Paseo Arts District is a creative enclave for artists and visitors alike. Tucked along two blocks of Spanish-revival and stucco buildings, the Paseo has retained the bohemian charm that has defined the neighborhood (originally a shopping district) since it was developed in the late 1920s.

Today, the Paseo is vibrant home to more than twenty galleries and eighty artists' studios and a trendy spot for live music, hole-in-the-wall cocktail lounges, and a very well-attended monthly gallery walk, First Friday, which showcases dozens of artists at several opening receptions in participating galleries.

If you're in OKC during Memorial Day weekend, make sure your plans include the annual Paseo Arts Festival, an Oklahoma City tradition for more than forty years, featuring three days of live music performances and artists from around the country.

NW 28th and Walker to NW 30th and Dewey, Oklahoma City
(405) 525-2688
thepaseo.org

RELIVE THE AMERICAN WEST

AT THE NATIONAL COWBOY AND WESTERN HERITAGE MUSEUM

The shortest distance between the modern day and the historic great American West is the National Cowboy and Western Heritage Museum. See American history unfold through one of the most comprehensive collections of Western art, artifacts, and sculptures in the world, beginning with the iconic and hauntingly beautiful James Earle Fraser sculpture, *The End of the Trail.*

Among the museum's many galleries, collections depict the stories of the American cowboy, settlers, Native Americans, the frontier military, rodeo performers, and famous Western performers of stage and screen. Kids will love Prosperity Junction, a turn-of-the-century replica cattle town.

Make time to visit the museum's beautiful gardens and pay your respects to the dearly departed animals (horses and bulls) in the rodeo animal cemetery. Their headstones are hilarious! Finally, do not miss the Museum Store, which boasts one of the state's largest collections of Native American-made jewelry, as well as fine apparel, accessories, home décor, Oklahoma-themed gifts, and books.

1700 NE 63rd St., Oklahoma City
(405) 478-2250
nationalcowboymuseum.org

TRAVEL TO THE LAND BEFORE TIME:
SAM NOBLE MUSEUM OF NATURAL HISTORY

Journey back to antiquity at the Sam Noble Museum of Natural History where five hundred million years of history come to life through the museum's extensive collection of ten million artifacts.

The museum is divided into five galleries that reveal Oklahoma's natural history, its thirty-thousand-year Native American history, its broad biodiversity of landscape, and the dinosaurs that used to roam its black mesa peaks and grasslands.

As you enter the museum, you'll be greeted by an Oklahoma native, the Sauroposeidon proteles, the world's tallest known dinosaur whose forty-foot-long neck and skull peer into the museum's Great Hall. Inside the Hall of Ancient Life, check out the magnificent, fully articulated skeleton of the Pentaceratops, whose 10.5-foot skull holds the Guinness World Record as the world's largest.

The Special Exhibitions Gallery welcomes various traveling exhibitions throughout the year.

Open daily (except on major holidays). Children under age seventeen are admitted free on the first Monday of the month.

2401 Chautauqua Ave., Norman (south side of the
University of Oklahoma campus)
(405) 325-4712
samnoblemuseum.ou.edu

77

MEET THE MASTERS
AT THE FRED JONES JR. MUSEUM OF ART

A highly respected university art museum, the Fred Jones Jr. Museum of Art on the University of Oklahoma campus gives visitors a unique opportunity to see important works by some of the best-known and most important artists of all time.

Highlights of the museum's offerings include the Weitzenhoffer Collection of French Impressionism, which features twenty-two paintings and eleven works on paper by such artists as Degas, Gauguin, Monet, Pissarro, Renoir, Toulouse-Lautrec, Van Gogh, Vuillard, and others.

The museum's collection consists of more than twenty-thousand objects, including major works by Ansel Adams, Romare Bearden, John Singleton Copley, Stuart Davis, Edward Hopper, early Kiowa artists, Maria Martinez, Georgia O'Keeffe, Ben Shahn, Edward Weston, and Oklahoma natives Olinka Hrdy, Allan Houser, and Leon Polk Smith.

Thanks to a gift from the OU Athletics Department that provides free admission to the museum in perpetuity, there is no charge for entry.

Closed on Mondays and on University holidays.

555 Elm Ave., Norman (OU campus)
(405) 325-3273
ou.edu/fjjma

TUNE INTO AMERICANA
AT THE AMERICAN BANJO MUSEUM

Tour an important part of America's musical history at the American Banjo Museum in Bricktown, where you'll see the world's largest collection of banjos on display.

Trace the banjo's roots as a handmade folk instrument and follow its rise as a beloved symbol of Americana through the museum's physical timeline, which highlights the minstrel era, the classic era, the Roaring '20s, and the modern era. Visit the on-site American Banjo Hall of Fame on the second floor to learn about the contributions of banjo pioneers, contemporary artists, manufacturers, and promoters who carry on the banjo's rich tradition, such as Bill Monroe and The Bluegrass Boys, The Kingston Trio, The Gibson Company, and Steve Martin. Don't miss seeing one of the most famous banjos of all time, the Muppets Banjo, which accompanied many of the weekly guest stars on The Muppet Show.

Want to learn to play the banjo? Join host Lucas Ross for a "Pick a Tune" class for absolute beginners one Saturday each month and learn to play a song before you leave. Banjos are provided. (Reservations required.) If you're ready to take your show on the road, you can buy a banjo in the gift store.

Closed Mondays.

9 E Sheridan Ave., Oklahoma City
(405) 604-2793
americanbanjomuseum.com

79

SEE WHAT'S NEXT
AT OKLAHOMA CONTEMPORARY

With a focus on living artists, the art of now, and the art of what's next, Oklahoma Contemporary Arts Center hosts free exhibitions, events, and performances year-round. Currently located in its longtime home at State Fair Park, Oklahoma Contemporary is on the brink of unveiling its new location, scheduled to open in fall 2019 at NW 11th Street and Broadway near downtown. The new facility promises to be a premier destination for exhibitions, performances, and education—a "creative commons" for the community to gather, create, and experience art.

3000 General Pershing Blvd.
(beginning fall 2019: NW 11th and Broadway), Oklahoma City
(405) 951-0000
oklahomacontemporary.org

ALL ABOARD
THE OKLAHOMA RAILWAY MUSEUM

See restored locomotives, a nineteenth-century depot, and memorabilia displays at the Oklahoma Railway Museum, one of the city's most unique educational attractions for train enthusiasts of all ages. Located in northeast Oklahoma City, this outdoor museum gives visitors a look at Oklahoma's railroad and street rail history.

The museum's exhibits include a variety of railcars, equipment, and railroad memorabilia. Climb aboard a real passenger train, see a real steam engine, visit a red caboose, a dining car, and a Pullman car. Then step inside a former Rock Island baggage car that was built in 1927, and view an expansive model train village.

You can even ride aboard a passenger train! Trains run the first and third Saturdays from April to August, the first Saturday in September, and the last Saturday in October. Admission to the Oklahoma Railway Museum is free.

Open Thursday, Friday, and Saturday 9:00 a.m. to 5:00 p.m. but may be closed due to inclement weather or temperatures below 40°F.

3400 NE Grand Blvd., Oklahoma City
(405) 424-8222
oklahomarailwaymuseum.org

CONFRONT YOUR FEARS
AT THE OKC RATTLESNAKE MUSEUM

Check your heebie-jeebies at the door and face your fears with a (safe) close-up look at some of the West's most dangerous snakes at the OKC Rattlesnake Museum.

The museum opened in 2018 in Oklahoma City's Stockyards City, giving visitors an opportunity to learn more about snakes, nature's most misunderstood creatures. Among the museum's twenty-six exhibits are about thirty-five venomous snakes and lizards. The museum features a selection of rattlesnakes from the United States (you'll feel the hair stand on the back of your neck when they all begin rattling in unison), including a creep-tastic albino western diamondback rattlesnake.

The museum's curator, Carl Sandefer, stays close by (thankfully) to answer questions about snakes and help visitors learn how to recognize which snakes are dangerous and which are not in the wild.

Open daily from 11:00 a.m. to 4:00 p.m. on weekdays and 10:00 a.m. to 4:00 p.m. on weekends. Admission is free.

1501 S Agnew Ave., Oklahoma City
(405) 850-5905
facebook.com/snakemuseumokc

82

EXPLORE, LEARN, AND PLAY
AT SCIENCE MUSEUM OKLAHOMA

With 350,000 square feet of cultural artifacts and interactive exhibits on space, aviation, art, and history, Science Museum Oklahoma is a sure bet to pique the curiosity of visitors of all ages.

It's probably impossible to do everything at the Science Museum in one day, but the newly updated Kirkpatrick Planetarium is an ideal place to start. Journey through the solar system and the farthest reaches of the universe or take a rollercoaster ride from the moon to the distant reaches of our galaxy. (Check website for show times; planetarium show admission is included in your general admission.)

Allow plenty of time to explore CurioCity (pronounced "curiosity"), a twenty-thousand-square-foot village with eight "neighborhoods" for interactive learning and play, like Tinker Works, where creative thinking and engineering design come together, or Wunderground, a cave-like space that includes obstacles, a dinosaur dig, and water play.

Finally, take a closer (and safer!) look at Oklahoma's extreme weather inside a tornado simulator in the Eye on the Sky exhibit.

2020 Remington Pl., Oklahoma City
(405) 602-6664
sciencemuseumok.org

WAGONS, HO!
AT THE CENTENNIAL LAND RUN MONUMENT

Hop onto a covered wagon or strike a pose with a statuesque settler at the Centennial Land Run Monument, a massive collection of forty-five bronze statues that pay tribute to the Land Run of 1889. Located along the south end of the city's Bricktown Canal and spanning a distance of 365 feet, the series of sculptures is the largest in the world. Created by Norman, Oklahoma, artist Paul Moore, whose great-grandfather participated in the 1889 Land Run, the display captures the energy, chaos, and determination surrounding the historic day in April 1889, when tens of thousands raced into the Unassigned Land in Oklahoma Territory to stake their claim to a new future in Oklahoma.

Admission to the park is free, with parking available just to the east of the monument. Enter at 200 Centennial Avenue, which is just off Reno Avenue, between Bass Pro Shop and the Residence Inn Hotel.

200 Centennial Ave., Oklahoma City
(405) 297-8912
landrun.marbleart.us

84

POINTES FOR STYLE:
OKC BALLET

The city's professional ballet company brings together talented native Oklahomans with ballet stars from around the world to form an inspired constellation of artistry and choreography on stage at the Civic Center Music Hall. The ballet stages about four classical and contemporary productions every year at the Civic Center. Among them is *The Nutcracker*, an Oklahoma City December tradition that includes The Nutcracker Tea, an opportunity for young patrons to meet and share treats with their favorite characters from the production.

6800 N Classen Ave., Oklahoma City
(405) 843-9898
okcballet.org

HIT ALL THE RIGHT NOTES
WITH THE OKLAHOMA CITY PHILHARMONIC

From September to May, the Civic Center Music Hall is your destination for masterful musical performances by the internationally acclaimed Oklahoma City Philharmonic. Sold-out audiences aren't uncommon during any of the classical and contemporary performances by the Phil, whose season includes eight classics performances and six "pops" productions, as well as three "Discovery Family Series," designed for children ages four to thirteen and their families. The "Discovery" concerts welcome children for pre-show activities, including a musical instrument playground, a conductor's corner, hands-on art creation, and more.

Following the 2018 retirement of its beloved music director Maestro Joel Levine, a thirty-year Philharmonic veteran, the Oklahoma City Philharmonic passes the baton to new music director Alexander Mickelthwate, whose aim is to inspire new emotions and insights with both the beloved masterpieces and new works to be performed by the Phil.

Civic Center Music Hall, 201 N Walker Ave., Oklahoma City
(405) 842-5387
okcphilharmonic.org

SEE THE CATTLE AUCTION
AT STOCKYARDS CITY

The Old West is alive and well just three miles south of downtown Oklahoma City. Modern day cowboys, horsemen, ranchers, and cattlemen go about their business every day in Stockyards City, a destination for authentic Western apparel, ranching equipment, and, of course, a good steak. If it's Monday or Tuesday morning, business as usual includes the cattle market, touted as the largest stocker and feeder cattle market in the world.

Nothing about Stockyards City is intentionally touristy, but tourists and locals alike are drawn to its collection of wooden front retail stores with merchandise that caters to real cowboys and cowgirls. Start at Mustang Creek Alpaca Company for locally raised alpaca wool products. If you don't own a real cowboy hat or a pair of cowboy boots, this is the place to find them. You'll discover a wide selection of boots, hats, western shirts (complete with pearl snaps), and more at Langston's Western Wear, Little Joe's Boots, and Shorty's Caboy Hattery, among others. Gear up and you'll be ready for Saturday night's live show at the Rodeo Opry.

2501 Exchange Ave., Oklahoma City
onsy.com

CELEBRATE NATIVE CULTURE
AT THE RED EARTH ART CENTER/ RED EARTH FESTIVAL

Experience Native American history through the works of various tribes at the Red Earth Art Center in downtown Oklahoma City, where the culture and traditions of the American Indian are beautifully articulated through more than fourteen hundred pieces of art on permanent display. Admission to the Art Center is free. A self-guided tour takes about forty-five minutes to an hour.

If you're visiting in June, don't miss the Red Earth Native American Cultural Festival, a celebration of visual and performing arts by about one hundred tribes. Dressed in full tribal regalia, more than twelve hunderd American Indian dancers participate in the Red Earth Pow Wow at the neighboring Cox Convention Center downtown. Sample Native American cuisine, view the works of some of the most talented Native artists in the US, and purchase art, pottery, paintings, jewelry, and more.

6 Santa Fe Plaza, Oklahoma City
(405) 427-5228
redearth.org

88

THE SKY'S THE LIMIT
AT THE NINETY-NINES MUSEUM OF WOMEN PILOTS

In the circa 1929 male-dominated field of aviation, women pilots faced opposition, criticism, and plenty of obstacles. In November 1929, a group of women pilots thumbed their collective noses at convention and decided to start an organization for female fliers, sending letters to the 117 women across the US who had their pilot's license. Of those 117, ninety-nine responded, giving the organization its name, the Ninety-Nines International Organization of Women Pilots. Amelia Earhart served as the Ninety-Nines' first president.

Today, the only museum dedicated to women fliers is housed on the second floor of the organization's headquarters, adjacent to Will Rogers World Airport, where you'll find a large collection of artifacts and displays that will take you through the history of the aviatrixes who charted their own courses to renown. On permanent display are Amelia Earhart's personal artifacts and memorabilia, as well as exhibits on Harriet Quimby, the first woman to receive a pilot's license in the US; Bessie Coleman, the first African American female pilot; and Sally Ride, the first American woman in space.

The museum offers guided tours, but requests about two weeks' notice to set one up.

4300 Amelia Earhart Rd., Oklahoma City
(405) 685-9990
museumofwomenpilots.org

89

KEEP YOUR EYE ON THE SKY
AT THE NATIONAL WEATHER CENTER

It's hard to spend time in Central Oklahoma without becoming fascinated by the weather here, and there's no better place to learn about it than at the Norman/Oklahoma City National Weather Service Weather Forecast Office and Storm Prediction Center, just south of the University of Oklahoma campus in Norman.

Public tours at the National Weather Center take place at 1:00 p.m. on Mondays, Wednesdays, and Fridays for a behind-the-scenes look at the center's premier facilities which contain the country's most advanced meteorology technology. In addition to the National Weather Service's forecast operation areas, you'll see the beehive of activity in the Storm Prediction Center, where all tornado and severe thunderstorm watches are issued for the contiguous forty-eight states. The University of Oklahoma School of Meteorology is also housed at the National Weather Center, along with the National Severe Storm Laboratory.

Tours are free, but you'll need to reserve your space in advance. Expect to spend an hour or an hour and a half. If you're there during breakfast or lunch, be sure to stop by the Flying Cow Café for a bite to eat.

120 David L. Boren Blvd., Norman
(405) 325-3095, ou.edu/nwc, weather.gov/oun

TIP

All tours require a reservation, which you'll want to make at least a week or two ahead of time. (No tours on federal or university holidays.) Photography is allowed, so bring your camera or smartphone!

The National Weather Center houses federal and university offices, so all related security procedures will be in place when you enter. (Leave your large purses, bags, and packages in the trunk of your car.) Parking is very convenient.

Photo courtesy of Cara Johnson for Blue Seven

SHOPPING AND FASHION

90

PLENTY TO LOVE
AT PLENTY MERCANTILE

The moment you cross the threshold of Plenty Mercantile, you'll know you've left the ordinary behind. This retail gem evokes an audible reaction ("Ohhhhhh, I looooooooove Plenty!") from anyone who has experienced its wonderfully curated collection of goods and products for every occasion. Readers of *405 Magazine* voted Plenty as "Best Home Accessories" store in 2018.

A retail shop bursting with unique and interesting items is a good thing, but Plenty operates at a much higher octave of goodness, offering only products—home décor, apparel, art, leather goods, vintage home accessories—that have been sustainably sourced. Shop owner Traci Walton considers it Plenty's mission to support product manufacturers who are thoughtful in their approach to fabrication. Plenty's inventory favors handcrafted items, with a preference for items that are made with renewable energy or that are organic, rescued, recycled, reusable, or biodegradable, or that have the philanthropic goal of improving the lives of others.

Plenty Mercantile has two locations:

Downtown/Automobile Alley
807 N Broadway Ave.
Oklahoma City
(405) 888-7470

Spring Creek Plaza
1466 S Bryant Ave., Edmond
(405) 888-9396

plentymercantile.com

JUMP-START THE FUN
AT JUMPIN' JACKALOPE MERCANTILE

Everyone's favorite Bricktown mercantile is a must-visit for Oklahoma-inspired gifts, tees and apparel, candy, handmade fudge, gourmet food and "artisan" jerky, home décor items, and jewelry. You could easily spend a couple of hours looking at all the unique treasures in this eclectic dry-goods-store-meets-Southwestern-chic-boutique.

Check your willpower at the door; you're bound to give in to the dozens of fudges, chocolates, truffles, and vintage candy. If you're in the mood for something more savory, take a tour of Jumpin' Jackalope's forty-eight bins of nuts and trail mixes and their impressive artisan selection of beef, venison, and buffalo jerky, available for purchase in bulk or packaged. Half the fun is in choosing among the all-star lineup of flavors, including hickory smoked, habañero and chili peppered, garlic, teriyaki, and one of the most popular options, whiskey barbecue.

208 Johnny Bench Dr., Oklahoma City (Bricktown)
(405) 673-7737
jumpinjackalope.com

92

YOUR NUMBER FOR RETAIL THERAPY

IS (BLUE) SEVEN (AND JUST OK)

Carve out some time because you're going to want to hang out all day in this locally owned apparel, home, and gift shop located in north Oklahoma City. Amply stocked with one-of-a-kind gifts, men's and women's apparel, shoes, home goods, Oklahoma-themed gifts, and so much denim, Blue Seven and its dedicated space for theme merchandise, Just OK, provide an effective dose of retail therapy. Even better, they're fully committed to promoting the Oklahoma-based companies, artists, and designers who create so many of the stores' top-quality products and jewelry, establishing a strong sense of connection and community between the customer and the designer. Readers of *405 Magazine* routinely call Blue Seven the best in the city for men's clothing and gifts (especially for the "impossible to buy for" recipient).

Blue Seven and Just OK
7518 N May Ave., Oklahoma City
(405) 604-5199
myblueseven.com

93

KEEPIN' IT LOCAL
AT DNA GALLERIES

This hybrid retail shop/contemporary art gallery is a driver for the revitalization of Oklahoma City's popular Plaza District. DNA's goal is to celebrate local artists and creativity in the community. There is a new featured art exhibit each month, so regular stops astthe store/gallery promise a different experience every time.

When you go, you'll appreciate the selection of unique, hand-crafted apparel and accessories, from T-shirts and handmade jewelry to the most hilarious greeting cards in the city. All of your Oklahoma-themed needs can be met right here, as well.

DNA Galleries is open seven days a week, but if you can time your visit to coincide with the second Friday of the month, you'll love mixing it up with locals during Live on the Plaza, the district's monthly block party (from 6:00 p.m. to 10:00 p.m.) that features live music, local shopping, various artists, and the best in food and drink.

1709 NW 16th St., Oklahoma City
(405) 525-3499
dnagalleries.com

SHOP GOOD
TO DO GOOD

"Changing the world one shirt at a time" has been the aim of Shop Good's owners, Justin and Audrey Falk, a husband and wife team who began designing and selling screen-printed tees at various festivals, with a desire to give back in the process. To do that, Shop Good partners with local charities, donating 5 percent of T-shirt sales to help meet needs within the community.

Today at Shop Good, you'll find so much more than the Falks' signature small-batch tees, including a carefully sourced collection of clothing, accessories, art and home décor, eyewear, jewelry, stationery and paper goods, and Oklahoma-centric apparel.

1007 N Broadway Ave., Oklahoma City
(405) 702-0517
shopgoodokc.com

YOUR FAVORITE THINGS LIVE

AT THE PAINTED DOOR GIFT BOUTIQUE

Rule #1: don't go to the Painted Door when you're short on time because you're going to want to savor this gift boutique. Go for the five-star Oklahoma-themed gifts and keepsakes you won't find elsewhere. Stay for everything else: jewelry, handbags, scarves, bath and body care, candles, home décor, gourmet foods, wedding gifts, women's and children's clothing and accessories, stationery, and a thousand other beautiful things you didn't realize you needed until that very moment. Even if you decide to stay all day, you can always count on superior customer service from the Painted Door's attentive staff. Closed Mondays.

124 E Sheridan Ave., Oklahoma City
(405) 235-4410
painteddoor.com

96

STAY ALL DAY
AT FULL CIRCLE BOOKS

Oklahoma's largest, independent, locally owned bookstore is also one of its most inviting spaces for exploring and discovering treasures from every genre among its more than sixty thousand titles. Whether you prefer to settle in for a good read by the fireplace with a glass of wine, champagne, or a locally brewed beer, or just to peruse the store's thirteen-foot, floor-to-ceiling bookcases (complete with ladders), you'll find it difficult to pull yourself away.

You won't find a better collection of books about Oklahoma or by Oklahoman authors than Full Circle's hand-selected titles, which include Native American books and several regional interest selections. Check the store's calendar of events. You'll always find offerings to engage the literary community, such as frequent book signings, poetry readings, Spanish classes, live music, and children's story time. In addition, the store's Garden Café is a must for any visit to Full Circle!

1900 Northwest Expy., Oklahoma City
(405) 842-2900
fullcirclebooks.com

Don't miss Pearl the Buffalo, a pearl-covered, semi-life-size bison statue, one of a herd of one hundred created by local artists as signature landmarks for businesses and notable locations in OKC. (Pearl is the only female in the herd.)

97

SHOP, DINE, PLAY
ON WESTERN AVENUE AND CLASSEN CURVE

Oklahoma City restaurateur and businessman Carl Milam, the unofficial "mayor of Western Avenue," once told me, "If you can't find it on Western Avenue, you don't need it." And he's right.

Spanning north from NW 36th Street to Wilshire Boulevard in northwest Oklahoma City, the Western Avenue District is the epitome of keeping things local, from restaurants of every culinary persuasion to funky boutique shopping, from antique stores to salons, from hole-in-the-wall dives to tony cocktail bars.

An important section of Western Avenue is the upscale Classen Curve. Anchored by this open-air center's crown jewel, Balliets, the Curve assembles the finest in designer fashion, accessories, and home décor in a central location with easy access and parking. The nearby Nichols Hills Plaza and The Triangle at Classen Curve touch all the retail bases with local boutiques and some of OKC's favorite dining spots.

Western Avenue District
N Western Avenue (from NW 36th Street to Wilshire Boulevard)
visitwesternavenue.com

Classen Curve
5825 NW Grand Blvd., Oklahoma City
(405) 902-2505
classencurve.com

GIFT-GIVING BEGINS
WITH ESSENTIALS

If it smells heavenly, it lives in Essentials, the city's hands-down favorite olfactory destination for exquisite candles, home fragrances, body lotions, premium bath and body products, and gifts everyone wants to receive. Located at Casady Square in northwest Oklahoma City, Essentials is a go-to for Nest, Aromatique, Crabtree & Evelyn, Trapp, Niven Morgan, Thymes, Lafco, and other top quality lines you won't see elsewhere in the OKC metro. Owner Georgana Morgan and her knowledgeable staff specialize in treating customers to personal (but not invasive) attention, and provide free samples with your purchase. You're sure to be inspired in your gift-giving, and it's worth the extra time to spend a few minutes finding the right card among Essentials' varied collection. Easy parking available right in front of the store.

9225 N Pennsylvania Pl. (SW corner of N Penn and Britton Road)
Oklahoma City
(405) 842-6401

UNCOMMONLY GOOD:
COMMONPLACE BOOKS

Normally, a recommendation about a retail enterprise relates to the products one might find, but customers at Commonplace Books in Oklahoma City's Midtown would attest to the store's inventory, selection, and customer service. I would add one more category to the mix: "restores your faith in humanity and everything that's right in the world."

A place that shares a common love for literature and people, Commonplace is anything but common with the value it places on the relationships with its customers (including a warm welcome from shop dog Boz). You're sure to appreciate any number of things about Commonplace's well-curated inventory and inviting, sit-a-spell atmosphere that may include live music, coffee and pastries to go with your newly purchased good read, or even a mixed drink or two, but don't miss sampling the menu from The Kitchen. Chris Castro is widely hailed as a culinary deity.

1325 N Walker Ave., Ste. 138, Oklahoma City
(405) 534-4540
commonplacebooksokc.com

100

SEE DESIGN COME TO LIFE
AT URBAN FARMHOUSE DESIGNS

In a world of immediate gratification and mass manufacturing, Urban Farmhouse Designs operates its entire business model on the premise that objects of value are still made by hand and that quality not only takes time, but stands the test of time.

As a locally owned, full-service manufacturer and retailer of residential and commercial furnishings and accessories created from reclaimed materials, Urban Farmhouse Designs specializes in one-of-a-kind pieces that celebrate a legacy and preserve the characteristics of enduring beauty and function. Each piece is manufactured on site in their incredible, fourteen-thousand-square-foot showroom by craftsmen who represent the best in their trade. Bring your design ideas with you or find inspiration in the store's showroom, or just come to watch the manufacturing, assembling, and finishing process right on site!

400 S Western Ave., Oklahoma City
(405) 812-8374
urbanfarmhouse.com

SUGGESTED ITINERARIES

DATE NIGHT

BRING THE KIDS

ADRENALINE ADVENTURE

MUSEUM CRAWL

MUSIC

ACTIVITIES
BY SEASON

SPRING

SUMMER

FALL

WINTER

INDEX

Photo courtesy of American Banjo Museum